Post Mortem
Essays, Historical
And Medical

by

C. MacLaurin

Post Mortem
Essays, Historical And Medical
by C. MacLaurin

ISBN: 978-93-59954-20-2

Published by

DOUBLE 9 BOOKS
2/13-B, Ansari Road
Daryaganj, New Delhi – 110002
info@double9books.com
www.double9books.com
Tel. 011-40042856

ABOUT THE AUTHOR

C. MacLaurin literary masterpiece, "Post Mortem," is a testament to his brilliance as a writer, seamlessly intertwining the realms of Mystery and Thriller. With meticulous attempt, MacLaurin crafts a story that not simplest captivates with its suspense however also fosters a profound connection among readers and the intricacies of the human revel in. His storytelling is going beyond more amusement, serving as a conduit for knowledge and empathy. A maestro of creativity and ardour, MacLaurin works transcend conventional limitations, taking readers on trips thru diverse landscapes of emotion. Whether exploring the enigmatic depths of a thriller or navigating the extreme thrills of a suspenseful plot, his writing exudes both beauty and accessibility. MacLaurin possesses the uncommon present of creating complicated narratives relatable, allowing an extensive target market to revel in the richness of his first-rate memories. In the world of C. MacLaurin, literature will become a bridge that connects human beings via shared studies, drawing them into the enthralling geographical regions he meticulously constructs. His potential to balance sophistication with approachability guarantees that everyone, no matter their literary options, can satisfaction in the magic woven into the material of his narratives.

CONTENTS

Preface

WHETHER the "great man" has had any real influence on the world, or whether history is merely a matter of ideas and tendencies among mankind, are still questions open to solution; but there is no doubt that great persons are still interesting; and it is the aim of this series of essays to throw such light upon them as is possible as regards their physical condition; and to consider how far their actions were influenced by their health. There are many remarkable people in history about whom we know too little to dogmatize, though we may strongly suspect that their mental and physical conditions were abnormal when they were driven to take actions which have passed into history; for instances, Mahomet and St. Paul. Such I have purposely omitted. But there were far more whose actions were clearly the result of their state of health; and some of these who happen to have been leaders at critical epochs I have ventured to study from the point of view of a doctor. This point of view appears to have been strangely neglected by historians and others. If the background against which it shows its heroes and heroines should appear unsentimental and harsh, at least it appears to medical opinion as probably true; and it is our duty to seek Truth. If it appears to assume an iconoclastic attitude towards many ideals I am sorry, and can only wish that the patina cast upon their characters were more sentimental and beautiful.

Jeanne d'Arc and the Emperor Charles V were undoubtedly heroic figures who have been almost worshipped by many millions of people; yet undoubtedly they were human and subject to the unhappy frailties of other people. This in no way detracts from their renown. I must apologize for treating Don Quixote as a real person; he was quite as much a living individual as anyone in history. Through his glamour we can get a real glimpse of the character of Cervantes.

In Australia we have no access to the original sources of European history; we must rely upon the "printed word" as it appears in standard monographs and essays.

I owe many thanks to Miss Kibble, of the research department of the Sydney Public Library, without whose help this work could never have been undertaken.

Sydney, 1922.

The Case of Anne Boleyn

THERE is something Greek, something akin to Œdipus and Thyestes, in the tragedy of Anne Boleyn. It is difficult to believe, as we read it, that we are viewing the actions of real people subject to passions violent indeed yet common to those of mankind, and not the creatures of a nightmare. Yet I believe that the conduct of the three protagonists, Henry, Catherine, and Anne, can all be explained if we appreciate the facts and interpret them with the aid of a little medical knowledge and insight. Let us search for this explanation. Needless to say we shall not get it in the strongly Bowdlerized sketches that most of us have learnt at school; it is a pity that such rubbish should be taught, because this period is one of the most important in English history; the actors played vital parts; and upon the drama that they played has depended the history of England ever since.

In considering an historical drama one has to remember the curtain of gauze which Time has drawn before us, and to allow for its colour and density. In the case of Henry VIII and his time, though the actual materials are enormous, yet everything has to be viewed through an *odium theologicum* that is unparalleled since the days of Theodora. In the eyes of the Catholics, Henry was, if not the actual devil incarnate, at all events the next thing; and their opinion has survived among many people who ought to know better to the present day. Decidedly we must make a great deal of allowance.

Henry succeeded to the throne, nineteen years of age, handsome, rather free-living, full of *joie-de-vivre*, charming, and with every promise of greatness and happiness. He died at fifty-five, unhappy, worn down with illness, at enmity with his people, with the Church, and with the world in general, leaving a memory in the popular mind of a murderous concupiscence that has become a byword. About the time that he was a young man, syphilis, which is supposed to have been introduced by Columbus' men, ran like a whirlwind through Europe. Hardly anyone seems to have escaped, and it was said that even the Pope upon the throne of St. Peter went the way of most other people, though it is possible that this accusation was as unreliable as many other accusations against the popes. Be that as it may, the foundations were then laid for that syphilization which has transformed the disease into its present mildness. It is impossible to doubt that Henry contracted it in his youth[1]; the evidence will become clear to any doctor as we proceed.

The first act of his reign was to marry for political reasons Catherine of Aragon, who was the widow of his elder brother Arthur. She was daughter of Ferdinand and Isabella of Spain, and, though far from beautiful, proved herself to possess a great and noble soul and a courage of well-tempered steel. The English people took her to their hearts, and when unmerited misfortune fell upon her never lost the love they had felt for her when she was a happy young woman. Though she was six years older than Henry, the two lived happily together for many years. Seven months after marriage Catherine was delivered of a daughter, still-born. Eight months later she had a son, who lived three days. Two years later she had a still-born son. Nine months later she had a son, who died in early infancy, and eighteen months afterwards the infant was born who was to live to be Queen Mary. Henry was intensely disappointed, and for the first time turned against his wife. It was all important to produce an heir to the throne, for it was thought that no woman could rule England. No woman had ever ruled England, save only Matilda, and her precedent was not alluring. So Henry longed desperately for a son; nevertheless as the little Mary grew up—a sickly child—he became passionately devoted to her. She grew up, as one can see from her well-known portrait, probably an hereditary syphilitic. For a time Henry had thought of divorcing Catherine, but his affection for Mary probably turned the scale in her mother's favour. Catherine had several more miscarriages, and by the time she was forty-two ceased to menstruate; it became clear that she would have no more children and could never produce an heir to the throne.

During these years Henry's morals had been no worse than those of any other prince in Europe; certainly better than Louis XIV and XV, who were to come after him, or Charles II. He met Mary Boleyn, daughter of a rich London merchant, and made her his mistress. Later on he met Anne Boleyn, her sister, a girl of sixteen, and fell in love. We have a very good description of her, and several portraits. She was of medium stature, not handsome, with a long neck, wide mouth, bosom "not much raised," eyes black and beautiful and a knowledge of how to use them. Her hair was long, and it appears that she used to wear it long and flowing in the house. It was not so very long since Joan of Arc had been burnt largely because she went about without a wimple, and Mistress Anne's conduct with regard to her hair was probably worse in those days than for a girl to be seen smoking cigarettes when driving a motor-car to-day. At any rate, she acquired demerit by it, and everybody was on the look-out for more serious false steps. The truth seems to be—so far as one can ascertain truth from reports which, even if unprejudiced, came from people who knew nothing about a woman's heart—that she was a bold and ambitious girl who laid herself out to capture Henry, and succeeded. Mary Boleyn was thrust aside, and Henry paid violent court in his own enormous and impassioned way to Anne. We have some of his love letters; there can be no doubt of his sincerity, or that his love for Anne was, while it lasted, the great passion of his life. Had she behaved herself she might have retained that love. She repulsed him for several years, and we can see the idea of divorce gradually growing in his mind. He appealed to Pope Clement VII to help him. Catherine defended herself bravely, and stirred Europe in her cause. The Pope hesitated, crushed between the hammer and the anvil, between Henry and the Emperor Charles V. Henry discovered that his marriage with Catherine had come within the prohibited degrees, and that she had never been his wife at all. It was a matter of doubt then—and I believe still is—whether the Pope's dispensation could acquit them of mortal sin. Apparently even his Holiness' influence would not have been sufficient to counterbalance the crime of marrying his deceased brother's widow; nevertheless it was rather remarkable that, if Henry were really such a stickler for the forms of canon law as he now wished to make out, he never troubled to raise the question until after he had fallen in love with some one else. He definitely promised Anne that he would divorce Catherine, marry Anne, and make her Queen of England. Secure in his promise, Anne yielded to her lover, seeing radiant visions of glory before her. How foolish would any girl be who let slip the chance—nay, the certainty—of being the Queen! Yet she was to discover that even queens can be bitterly unhappy. Anne sprang joyfully into the unknown, as many a girl has done before her and since, trusting to her power to charm her lover; and became pregnant. Meanwhile the struggle for the divorce proceeded, the Pope swaying this way and that, and Catherine defending her honour and her throne with splendid courage. The nurses and astrologers declared that the fœtus was a son, and the lovers, mad with joy, were married in secret, divorce or no divorce. The obliging Archbishop Cranmer pronounced that the marriage with Catherine was null and void, as the Pope would not do so.

The time came for Anne to fulfil her promise and provide an heir. King and queen anticipated the event in the wildest excitement. There had been several lovers' quarrels, which had been made up in the usual manner; once Henry was heard to say passionately that he would rather beg his bread in the streets than desert her. Yet it is doubtful whether Anne Boleyn was ever anything more than an ambitious courtesan; it is doubtful whether she ever felt anything towards him but her natural wish to be queen. In due course her baby was born, and it was a girl—the girl who afterwards became Queen Elizabeth.

Henry's disappointment was tragic, and for the first time Anne began to realize the terror of her position. She was detested by the people and the Court, who were emphatically on the side of the noble woman whom she had supplanted. She had estranged everybody by her vain-glory and arrogance in the hour of her triumph; and it began to be whispered that even if her own marriage were legal while Catherine was still alive, yet it was illegal by the canon law, for Mary Boleyn, her sister, had been Henry's wife in all but name. Canonically speaking, Henry had done no better by marrying her than by marrying Catherine. A horrible story went around that he had been familiar with her mother first, and that Anne was his own daughter, and moreover that he knew it. I think we can definitely and at once put this aside as an ecclesiastical lie; there is absolutely no evidence for it and it is impossible to conceive two persons more unlike than the little lively brunette and the great fresh-faced "bluff King Hal." Moreover, Henry denied the story absolutely, and whatever else he was, he was a man who was never afraid to tell the truth. Most of the difficulties in understanding this complex period of our history disappear if we believe Henry's own simple statements; but these suffer from the incredulity which Bismarck found three hundred years later when he told his rivals the plain unvarnished truth.

Let us anticipate events a little and narrate the death of Catherine, which took place in 1536, nearly three years after the birth of Elizabeth. The very brief and sketchy accounts which have survived give me the impression that she died of uræmia, but no definite opinion can be given. Henry, of course, lay under the immediate charge of having poisoned her, but I do not know that anybody believed it very seriously. So died this unhappy and well-beloved lady, to whom life meant little but a series of bitter misfortunes.

After Elizabeth was born the tragedy began to move with terrible impetus towards its climax. Henry developed an intractable ulcer on his thigh, which persisted till his death, and frequently caused him severe agony whenever the sinus closed. He became corpulent, the result of over-eating and over-drinking. He had been immensely worried for years over the affair of Catherine; as a result his blood-pressure seems to have risen, so that he was affected by frightful headaches, which often incapacitated him from work for days together. He gave up the athleticism which had distinguished his resplendent youth, aged rapidly, and became a harassed, violent, ill-tempered middle-aged man—not at all the sort of man to turn into a cuckold.

Yet this is precisely what Anne did. Less than a month after Elizabeth was born—while she was still in the puerperal state—she solicited Sir Henry Norreys, the most intimate friend of the King, to be her lover. A week later, on October 17th, 1533, he yielded. During the next couple of years Anne seems to have gone absolutely out of her senses, if the contemporary stories are true. She seems to have solicited several prominent men of the Court, and even to have stooped to one of the musicians; worst of all, it was said that she had committed incest with her brother, Lord Rocheford. Nor did she behave with the ordinary consideration for the feelings of others that might have brought her hosts of friends—remember, she was a queen!—should the time ever come when she should need them. It does not require any great amount of civility on the part of a queen to win friends. Arrogant and overbearing, she estranged everybody at Court; she acted like a beggar on horseback, and was left without a friend in the place. And she, who owed her husband such a world, behaved towards him with the same arrogance as she showed to others, and in addition jealousy both concerning other women whom she feared and concerning the King's beloved daughter, Mary. She spoke to the Duke of Norfolk—her uncle on the mother's side, and one of the greatest peers of the realm—"like a dog"; as he turned away he muttered that she was "une grande putaine." The most polite interpretation of the French word is "strumpet." When the Duke used such a word to his own niece, what sort of reputation must have been gathering about her?

She had two more miscarriages. After the second the King's fury flamed out, and he told her plainly that he deeply regretted having married her. He must have indeed been sorry; he had abandoned a good woman for a bad; for her he had quarrelled with the Pope and with many of his subjects; whatever conscience he had must have been tormenting him: all these things for the sake of an heir, which seemed as hopelessly unprocurable as ever. Both the women seemed affected by some fate which condemned them to perpetual miscarriages; this fate, of course, was Henry's own syphilis, even supposing that neither wife had contracted it independently. (It is much to Anne Boleyn's credit or discredit, that to a syphilitic husband she bore a daughter so vigorous as Elizabeth, though Professor Chamberlin does not appear to think very highly of her health.)

Meanwhile all sorts of scandalous rumours were flying about; and finally a maid of honour, whose chastity had been impugned, told a Privy Councillor that no doubt she herself was no better than she should be, but that at any rate her Majesty Queen Anne was far worse. The Privy Councillor related this to Thomas Cromwell; he, the rumours being thus focussed, dared to tell the King. Henry changed colour, and ordered a secret inquiry to be held. At this inquiry the ladies of the bedchamber were strictly cross-examined, but nothing was allowed to happen for a few days, when a secret commission was appointed, consisting of the Chancellor, the judges, Thomas Cromwell, and other members of the Council. Sir William Brereton was first sent to the Tower, then the musician Smeaton. Next day there was a tournament at Greenwich, in the midst of which Henry suddenly rose and left the scene, taking Norreys with him. Anne was brought before the Commission next day, and committed to the Tower, where she found that Sir Francis Weston had preceded her. Lord Rocheford, her brother, joined her almost immediately on the charge of incest.

The Grand Juries of Kent and Middlesex returned true bills on the cases, and the Commission drew up an indictment, giving names, places, and dates for every alleged act. The four commoners were put on trial at Westminster Hall. Anne's father, Lord Wiltshire, though he volunteered to sit, was excused attendance, since a verdict of guilty against the men would necessarily involve his daughter. One may read this either way, against or in favour of Anne. Either Wiltshire was enraged at her folly, and merely wished to end her disgrace; or it may be that he thought he would be able to sway the Court in her favour. Possibly he was afraid of the King and wished to show that he at least was on his royal side, however badly Anne may have behaved. In dealing with a harsh and tyrannical man like Henry VIII it is difficult to assess human motives, and one prefers to think that Wiltshire was trying to do his best for his daughter. Smeaton the musician confessed under torture; the other three protested their innocence, but were found guilty and were sentenced to death. Thomas Cromwell, in a letter, said that the evidence was so abominable that it could not be published. Evidently the Court of England had suddenly become squeamish.

Anne was next brought to trial before twenty-five peers of the realm, her uncle the Duke of Norfolk being in the chair. Probably, if the story just related were true, the Duke's influence would not be exerted very strongly in her favour, and she was convicted and sentenced to be hanged or burnt at the King's pleasure; her brother was tried separately and also convicted. It is said that her father and uncle concurred in the verdict; they may have been afraid of their own heads. On the other hand, it is possible that Anne was really guilty; unfortunately the evidence has perished. The five men were executed on Tower Hill in the presence of the woman, whose death was postponed from day to day. In the meantime Henry procured his divorce from her, while Anne, in a state of violent hysteria, continuously protested her innocence. On the night before her execution she said that the people would call her "Queen Anne sans tête," laughing wildly as she spoke; if one pronounces these words in the French manner, without verbal accent, they form a sort of jingle, as who should say "ta-ta-ta-ta"; and this foolish jingle seems to have run in her head, as she kept repeating it all the evening; and she placed her fingers around her slender neck—almost her only beauty— saying that the executioner would have little trouble, as though it were a great joke. These things were put to the account of her light and frivolous nature, and have probably weighed heavily with posterity in attempting to judge her case; but it is clear that they were merely manifestations of hysteria. Joan of Arc, whose character was probably the direct antithesis of Anne Boleyn's, laughed when she heard the news of her reprieve. Some people think she laughed ironically, as though a very simple peasant-girl could be ironical if she tried. Irony is a quality of the higher intelligence. But cannot a girl be allowed to laugh hysterically for joy? Or cannot Anne Boleyn be allowed to laugh hysterically for grief and terror without being called light and frivolous? So little did her contemporaries understand the human heart. A few years later came one Shakespeare, who could have told King Henry differently; and the extraordinary burgeoning forth of the English intellect in William Shakespeare is one of the most wonderful things in our history. Before the century had terminated in which Anne Boleyn had been considered light and frivolous because she had laughed in the shadow of the block, Shakespeare had plumbed the depths of human nature.

Anne was beheaded on May 19th, 1536, in the Tower, on a platform covered thickly with straw, in which lay hidden a broadsword. The headsman was a noted expert brought over specially from St. Omer, and he stood motionless among the gentlemen onlookers until the necessary preliminaries had been completed. Then, Anne kneeling in prayer and her back being turned towards him, he stole silently forward, seized the sword from its hiding-place, and severed her slender neck at a blow. As she had predicted, he had little trouble, and she never saw either her executioner or the sword that slew her.[2] Her body and severed head were bundled into a cask, and were buried within the precincts of the Tower; and Henry threw his cap into the air for joy. On the same day he obtained a special dispensation to marry Jane Seymour. He married her next day.

The chief authority for the reign of Henry VIII is contained in the *Letters and Papers of the Reign of Henry VIII*, edited by Brewer and Gairdner. This gigantic work, containing more than 20,000 closely printed pages, is probably the greatest monument of English scholarship; the prefaces to the different volumes are remarkable for their learning and delightful literary style. Froude's history is charming and brilliant as are all his writings, but is now rather out of date, and is marred by his hero-worship of Henry and his strong Protestant bias. He sums up absolutely against Anne, and, after reading the letters which he publishes, I do not see how he could have done anything else. He believes her innocent of incest, however, and doubtless he is right. Let us acquit her of this crime, at any rate. A. F. Pollard's *Life of Henry VIII* is meticulously accurate, and is charmingly written; he thinks it impossible that the juries could have found against her and the court have convicted without the strongest evidence, which has not survived. P. C. Yorke sums up rather against her in the *Encyclopædia Britannica*; but S. R. Gardiner thinks the charges too horrible to be believed and that probably her own only offence was that she could not bear a son. Professor Gardiner had evidently seen little of psychological medicine, or he would have known that no charge is too horrible to believe. The "Unknown Spaniard" of the *Chronicle of Henry VIII* is an illiterate fellow enough, but no doubt of Anne's guilt appears to enter his artless mind; he probably represents the popular contemporary view. He says that he took his stand in the ring of gentlemen who witnessed the execution. He gives an account of the arrest of Sir Thomas Wyatt the poet—the first English sonneteer—and the *ipsissima verba* of a letter which Wyatt wrote to Henry, narrating how Anne had solicited him even before her marriage in circumstances that rendered her solicitation peculiarly brazen and shameless. That Henry should have pardoned him seems to show that the real crime of Anne was that she had contaminated the blood royal; a capital offence in a queen in almost all ages and almost every country. Before she became a queen Henry was probably complaisant enough to Anne's peccadilloes; but afterwards—that was altogether different. "There's a divinity doth hedge" a queen!

Lord Herbert of Cherbury, writing seventy years later, narrates the ghastly story with very little feeling one way or the other. Apparently the legend of Anne's innocence and Henry's blood-lust had not yet arisen. The verdict of any given historian appears to depend upon whether he favours the Protestants or the Catholics. Speaking as a doctor with very little religious preference one way or the other, the following considerations appeal strongly to myself. If Henry wished to get rid of a barren wife— barren through his own syphilis!—as he undoubtedly did, then Mark Smeaton's evidence alone was enough to hang any queen in history from Helen downward, especially if taken in conjunction with the infamous stories related by the "Unknown Spaniard." Credible or not, these stories show the reputation that attached to the plain little Protestant girl who could not provide an heir to the throne—the sort of reputation which mankind usually attaches to a woman who, by unworthy means, has attained to a high position. Why should the King and Cromwell, both exceedingly able men, gratuitously raise the questions of incest and promiscuity and send four innocent men to their deaths absolutely without reason? Why should they raise all the tremendous family ill-will and public reprobation which such an act of bloodthirsty tyranny would have caused? Stern as they were they never showed any sign of mere blood-lust at any other time; and the facts that Anne's father and uncle both appear to have concurred in the verdict, and that, except for her own denial, there is not a word said in her favour, seems to require a great deal of explanation.

We can thoroughly explain her conduct by supposing that she was afflicted by hysteria and nymphomania. There are plenty of accounts of unhappy women whose cases are parallel to Anne's in the works of Havelock-Ellis and Kisch. There is plenty of indubitable evidence that she was hysterical and unbalanced, and that she passionately longed for a son; and it is simpler to believe her the victim of a well-known and common disease than that we should suppose the leading statesmen of England and nearly the whole of its peerage suddenly to be affected with blood-lust. It has been suggested that Anne, passionately longing for a son and terrified of her husband's tyrannical wrath, acted like one of Thomas Hardy's heroines centuries later and tried another lover in the hope that she would gratify her own and Henry's wishes. This course of procedure is probably not so uncommon as some husbands imagine and would satisfy the questions of our problem but for Anne's promiscuity and vehemence in solicitation. If her sole object in soliciting Norreys was to provide a son, why should she have gone from man to man till the whole Court seems to have been ringing with her ill fame?

Her spasms of violent temper after her marriage, her fits of jealousy, her foolish arrogance and insolence to her friends, are all mental signs which go with nymphomania, and the fact that her post-nuptial incontinence seems to have begun while she was still in the puerperal state after the birth of her only living child seems highly significant. It is not uncommon for sexual desire to become intolerable in nervous and puerperal women. The proper place for Anne Boleyn was a mental hospital.

Henry VIII's case, along with those of his children, deserve a paper to themselves. Henry himself died of neglected arterio-sclerosis just in the nick of time to save the lives of better men from the executioner; Catherine Parr, who married him probably in order to nurse him—it is possible that she was really fond of him and that there was even then something attractive about him—succeeded in outliving him by a remarkable effort of diplomatic skill and courage, though had Henry awakened from his uræmic stupor probably her head would have been added to his collection. On the whole, one cannot avoid the conclusion that his conduct to his wives was not all his fault. They seem to have done no credit to his power of selection. The first and the last appear to have been the best, considered as women.

Inexorable Nemesis had avenged Catherine. The worry of the divorce left her husband with an arterial tension which, added to the royal temper, caused great misery to England and ultimately death to himself; and her mean little rival lay huddled in the most frightful dishonour that ever befell a woman. Decidedly there is something Greek in the complete horror of the tragedy.

The Problem of Jeanne d'Arc

IN 1410-12 France was in the most dreadful condition that has ever affected any nation. For nearly eighty years England had been at her throat in a quarrel which to our minds simply exemplifies the difference between law and justice; for it seems that the King of England had mediæval law on his side, though to our minds no justice; the Black Death had returned more than once to harass those whom war had spared; no man reaped where he had sown, for his crops fell into the hands of freebooters. Misery, destitution, and superstition were man's bedfellows; and the French mind seemed open to receive any marvel that promised relief from its intolerable agony. Into this land of terror was born a little maid whose mission it was to right the wrongs of France; a maiden who has remained, through all the vicissitudes of history, extraordinarily fascinating, yet an almost insoluble pròblem. It is undeniable that she has exercised a vast influence upon mankind, less by her actual deeds than by the ideal which she set up; an ideal of courage, simple faith, and unquenchable loyalty which has inspired both her own nation and the nation which burnt her. When the English girls cut their hair short in the worst time of the war;[3] when the French soldiers retook Fort Douaumont when all seemed lost: these things were done in the name of Joan of Arc.

The actual contemporary sources from which we draw our ideas are extraordinarily few. There is of course the report of the trial for lapse and relapse, which is official and is said not to be garbled. It is useful, not only for the Maid's answers, which throw a good deal of light on her mentality, but for the questions asked, which appear to give an idea of reports that seem to have been floating about France at the time. The only thing which interested her judges was whether she had imperilled her immortal soul by heresy or witchcraft, and from that trial we shall get few or no indications of her military career or physical condition, which are the things that most interest modern men. About twenty years after her execution it occurred to her king, who had repaid her amazing love and self-sacrifice with neglect, that since she had been burnt as a witch it followed that he must owe his crown to a witch; moreover, her mother and brother had been appealing to him to clear her memory, for they could not bear that their child and sister should still remain under a cloud of sorcery. King Charles VII, who was now a great man, and very successful as kings go, therefore ordered the case to be reopened, in which course he ultimately secured the assistance of the reigning Pope. Charles could not restore the Maid to life, but he could make things unpleasant for the friends of those who had burned her; and so we have the so-called Rehabilitation Trial, consisting of reports and opinions, given under oath, from many people who had known her when alive. As King Charles was now a great man, some of the clerics who had helped to condemn her crowded to give evidence in the poor child's favour, attributing the miscarriage of justice in her case to people who were now dead or hopelessly unpopular; some friends of her childhood came forward and people who had known her at the time of her glory; and, perhaps most important, some of her old comrades in arms rallied round her memory. We thus have a fairly complete account of her battles, friendships, trials, character, and death; if we read this evidence with due care, remembering that more than twenty years had elapsed and the mentality of mediæval man, we may take some of the statements at their face value. Otherwise there is absolutely no contemporary evidence of the Maid; Anatole France has pricked the bubble of the chroniclers and of the Journal of the siege of Orleans. But there is so much of pathological interest to be found in the reports of the trials that I need no excuse for a brief study of them in that respect.

The record of the life of Jeanne d'Arc is all too short, and the main facts are not in dispute. It is the interpretation of these facts that *is* in dispute. She was born on January 6th, 1412; the year is uncertain. Probably she did not know herself. In the summer of 1424 she saw a great light on her right hand and heard a voice telling her to be a good girl. This voice she knew to be the voice of God. Later on she heard the voices of St. Michael the Archangel, of St. Catherine, and of St. Margaret. St. Michael appeared first, and warned her to expect the arrival of the others, who came in due course. All three were to be her constant companions for the rest of her life. At first their appearances were irregular, but later on they came frequently, especially at quiet moments. Sometimes, when there was a good deal of noise going on, they appeared and tried to tell her something, but she could not hear what they said. These she called her Council, or her Voices. Occasionally the Lord God spoke to her himself; Him she called "Messire."

As Jeanne grew more accustomed to her heavenly visitors they came in great numbers, and she used to see vast crowds of angels descending from heaven to her little garden. She said nothing to anybody about these unusual events, but grew up a brooding and intensely religious girl, going to church at every possible opportunity, and apparently neglecting her ordinary duties of looking after her father's sheep and cattle. She learned to sew and knit, to say her Credo, Paternoster, and Ave Maria; otherwise she was absolutely ignorant, and very simple in mind and honest. She was dreamy and shy; nor did she ever learn to read or write.

Later on the voices told her to go into France, and God would help her to drive out the English. She continually appealed to her father that he should send her to Vaucouleurs, where the Sieur Robert de Baudricourt would espouse her cause. Ultimately he did so; and at first Robert laughed at her. He was no saint; in his day he had ravaged villages with the best noble in the land; and he was not convinced that Jeanne was really the sent of God that she claimed. When she returned home she found herself the butt of Domremy; nine months later she ran away to Vaucouleurs again, and found Robert more helpful. He had for some time felt sympathy with the dauphin Charles, and had grown to detest the English and Burgundians; and he now welcomed the supernatural aid which Jeanne promised; she repeated vehemently that God had sent her to deliver France, and that she had no doubt whatever that she would be able to raise the siege of Orleans, which was then being idly invested by the English.

Robert sent her to the Dauphin, who lay at Chinon. He was no hero, this Dauphin, but a poverty-stricken ugly man, with spindle-shanks and bulbous nose, untidy and careless in his dress, and for ever blown this way and that by the advice of those around him. Weak, and intensely superstitious, he would to-day have been the prey of every medium who cared to attack him; he received Jeanne kindly, and ultimately sent her to Poitiers to be examined as to possible witchcraft by a great number of learned doctors of the Church, who could be relied upon to discern a witch as soon as anybody.

She was deeply offended at being suspected of witchcraft, and was not so respectful to her judges as she might have been; occasionally she sulked, and sometimes she answered the reverend gentlemen quite saucily. She is an attractive and very human little figure at Poitiers as she moves restlessly upon her bench, and repeatedly tells the doctors that they should need no further sign than her own deeds; for when she had relieved Orleans it would be obvious enough that she was sent directly from God. At Poitiers she had to run the gauntlet of the inevitable jury of matrons, who were to certify to her virginity, because it was well known that women lost their holiness when they lost their virginity. The matrons and midwives certified that she was *virgo intacta*; how the good ladies knew is not certain, because even to-day, with all our knowledge of anatomy and physiology, we often find it difficult to be assured on this point. However, there can be little doubt that they were correct; probably they were impressed with Jeanne's obvious sincerity and purity of mind. All women seem to have loved Jeanne, which is a strong point in her favour. The spiritual examination dragged on for three weeks; these poor doctors were determined not to let a witch slip through their hands, and it speaks well for their patience and good temper, considering how unmercifully Jeanne had "cheeked" them, that they ultimately found that she was a good Christian. Any ordinary man would have seen that at once; but these gentlemen knew too much about the wiles of the Devil to be so easily influenced; and it was a source of bitter injustice to Jeanne at her real and serious trial for her life that she was unable to produce their certificate.

The Dauphin took her into his service and provided her with horse, suit of armour, and banner, as befitted a knight; also maidservants to act propriety, page-boy, and a steward, one Jean d'Aulon. All that we hear of d'Aulon, in whose hands the honour of the Maid was placed, is to his credit. A witness at the Rehabilitation Trial said that he was the wisest and bravest man in the army. We shall hear more of him. Throughout the story, whenever he comes upon the scene we seem to breathe fresh air. He was the very man for the position, brave, simple-hearted, and passionately loyal to Jeanne. There is no reason to doubt that in spite of his close companionship with her there was never any romantic or other such feeling between them; he said so definitely, and he is to be believed. His honour came through it all unstained; and he let himself be captured with her rather than desert her. It is clear from his evidence that the personality of the Maid profoundly affected him. After Jeanne's death he was ransomed, and was made seneschal of Beaucaire.

Jeanne was enormously impressed by her banner, which was made by a Scotsman, Hamish Power by name; she described it at her trial.

"I had a banner of white cloth, sprinkled with lilies; the world was painted there, with an angel on each side; above them were the words 'Jhesus Maria.'" When she said "the world" she meant God holding the world up in one hand and blessing it with the other. Later on she does not seem very certain whether "Jhesus Maria" was above or at the side; but she is very certain that she was tremendously proud of the artistic creation— yes, "forty times" prouder of her banner than of her sword; even though the sword was from St. Catherine herself, and was the very sword of Charles Martel centuries before. When the priests dug it up without witnesses and rubbed it their holy power cleansed it immediately of the rust of ages.

When she arrived at Orleans she found the English carrying on a leisurely blockade by means of a series of forts between which cattle and men could enter or leave the city at will. The city was defended by Jean Dunois, Bastard of Orleans. The title Bastard implies that he would have been Duc d'Orleans only that he had the misfortune to be born of the wrong mother. There have been several famous bastards in history, and the kindly morality of the Middle Ages seems to have thought little the worse of them for their misfortune. It is only fair to state that there is some doubt as to whether Jeanne was sent in command of the army, or the army in command of Jeanne; indeed, all through her story it is never easy to be certain whether she was actually in command, and Anatole France looks upon her as a sort of military *mascotte* rather than a soldier. Nor has Anatole France ever been properly answered. Andrew Lang did his best, as Don Quixote did his best to fight the windmills, but Mr. Lang was an idealist and romanticist, and could not defeat the laughing irony of M. France. Indeed, what answer is possible? Anatole France does not laugh at the poor little Maid; he laughs through her at modern French clericalism. Nobody with a heart in his breast could laugh at Jeanne d'Arc! Anatole France simply said that he did not believe the things which Mr. Lang said that he believed; he would be a brave man who should say that M. France is wrong.

When she reached Orleans a new spirit at once came into the defenders, just as a new spirit came into the British army on the Somme when the tanks first went forth to battle—a spirit of renewed hope; God had sent his Maid to save the right! In nine days of mild fighting, in which the French enormously outnumbered the English, the siege was raised. The French lost a few score men; the English army was practically destroyed.

Next Jeanne persuaded the Dauphin to be crowned at Rheims, which was the ancient crowning-place for the French kings. In this ancient cathedral, in whose aisles and groined vaults echoed the memories and glories of centuries, he was crowned; his followers standing around in a proud assembly, his adoring peasant-maid holding her grotesque banner over his head; probably the most extraordinary scene in all history. After Jeanne had secured the crowning of her king, ill-fortune was thenceforth to wait upon her. She was of the common people, and it was only about eighty years since the aristocracy had shuddered before the herd during the Jacquerie, the premonition of the Revolution of 1789. Class feeling ran strongly, and the nobles took their revenge; Jeanne, having no ability whatever beyond her implicit faith in Heaven, lost her influence both with the Court and with the people; whatever she tried to do failed, and she was finally captured in a sortie from Compiêgne in circumstances which do not exclude the suspicion that she was deliberately sacrificed. The Burgundians held her for ransom, and locked her up in the Tower of Beaurevoir. King Charles VII refused—or at any rate neglected—to bid for her; so the Burgundians sold her to the English. When she heard that she was to be given into the hands of her bitterest enemies she was so troubled that she leaped from the tower, a height of sixty or seventy feet, and was miraculously saved from death by the aid of her friends—Saints Margaret and Catherine. It is easier to believe that at her early age—she was then about nineteen or possibly even less— her epiphyseal cartilages had not ossified, and if she fell on soft ground it is perfectly credible that she might not receive worse than a severe shock. I remember a case of a child who fell from a height of thirty feet on to hard concrete, which it struck with its head; an hour later it was running joyfully about the hospital garden, much to the disgust of an anxious charge-nurse. It is difficult to kill a young person by a fall—the bones and muscles yield to violent impact, and life is not destroyed.

Jeanne having been bought by the English they brought her to trial before a court composed of Pierre Cauchon, Lord Bishop of Beauvais, and a varying number of clerics; as Anatole France puts it, "a veritable synod"; it was important to condemn not only the witch of the Armagnacs herself but also the viper whom she had been able to crown King of France. If they condemned her for witchcraft they condemned all her works, including King Charles. If Charles had been a clever man he would have foreseen such a result and would have bought her from the Duke of Burgundy when he had the chance. But when she was once in the iron grip of the English he could have done nothing. It was too late. If he had offered to buy her the English would have said she was not for sale; if he had moved his tired and disheartened army they would have handed her over to the University of Paris, or perhaps the dead body of one more peasant-girl would have been found in the Seine below Rouen, and Cauchon would have been spared the trouble of a trial. Therefore we may spare our regrets on the score of some at least of King Charles's ingratitudes. It is possible that he did not buy her from the Burgundians because he was too stupid, too poor, or too parsimonious; it is more likely that his courtiers and himself began to believe that her success was so great that it could not be explained by mortal means, and that there must be something in the witchcraft story after all. It could not have been a pleasant thing for the French aristocrats to find that when a little maid from Domremy came to help the common people, these scum of the earth suddenly began to fight as they had not fought for generations. Fully to understand what happened we must remember that it was not very long since the Jacquerie, and that the aristocratic survivors had left to their sons tales of unutterable horrors.

However, Jeanne was put on her trial for witchcraft, and after a long and apparently hesitating process—for there had been grave doubts raised as to the legality of the whole thing—she was condemned to death. Just before the Bishop had finished his reading of the sentence she burst into tears and recanted, when she really understood that they were even then preparing the cart to take her to the stake. She said herself, in words which cannot possibly be misunderstood, that she recanted "for fear of the fire."

The sentence of the court was then amended; instead of being burned she was to be held in prison on bread and water and to wear woman's clothes. She herself thought that she was to be put into an ecclesiastical prison and be kept in the charge of women, but there is nothing to be found of this in the official report of the first trial. As she had been wearing men's clothes by direct command of God her sin in recanting began to loom enormous before her during the night; she had forsaken her God even as Peter had forsaken Jesus Christ in the hour of his need, and hell-fire would be her portion — a fire ten thousand times worse than anything that the executioner could devise for her. She got up in the morning and threw aside the pretty dress which the Duchess of Bedford had procured for her — all women loved Jeanne d'Arc — and put on her war-worn suit of male clothing. The English soldiers who guarded her immediately spread abroad the bruit that Jeanne had relapsed, and she was brought to trial for this contumacious offence against the Holy Church. The second trial was short and to the point; she tried to show that her jailers had not kept faith with her, but her pleadings were brushed aside, and finally she gave the *responsio mortifera* — the fatal answer — which legalized the long attempts to murder her. Thus spoke she: "God hath sent me word by St. Catherine and St. Margaret of the great pity it is, this treason to which I have consented to abjure and save my life! I have damned myself to save my life! Before last Thursday my Voices did indeed tell me what I should do and what I did then on that day. When I was on the scaffold on Thursday my Voices said to me: 'Answer him boldly, this preacher!' And in truth he is a false preacher; he reproached me with many things I never did. If I said that God had not sent me I should damn myself, for it is true that God has sent me; my Voices have said to me since Thursday: 'Thou hast done great evil in declaring that what thou hast done was wrong.' All I said and revoked I said for fear of the fire."

To me this is the most poignant thing in the whole trial, which I have read with a frightful interest many times. It seems to bring home the pathos of the poor struggling child, and her blind faith in things which could not help her in her hour of sore distress.

Jules Quicherat published a very complete edition of the Trial in 1840, which has been the basis for all the accounts of Jeanne d'Arc that have appeared since. An English translation was published some years ago which professed to be complete and to omit nothing of importance. But this work was edited in a fashion so vehemently on Jeanne's side, with no apparent attempt to ascertain the exact truth of the judgments, that I ventured to compare it with Quicherat, and I have found some omissions which to the translator, as a layman, may have seemed unimportant, but which, to a doctor, seem of absolutely vital importance in considering the truth about the Maid. These omissions are marked in the English by a row of three dots, which might be considered to mark an omission,—but on the other hand might not. Probably the translator considered them too indecent, too earthly, too physiological, to be introduced in connexion with the Maid of God. But Jeanne had a body, which was subject to the same peculiarities and abnormalities as the bodies of other people; and upon the peculiarities of her physiology depended the peculiarities of her mind.

Jean d'Aulon, her steward and loyal admirer, said definitely in the Rehabilitation Trial, in 1456:—

"Qu'il oy dire a plusiers femmes, qui ladicte Pucelle ont veue par plusiers foiz nues, et sceue de ses secretz, que oncques n'avoit eu la secret maladie de femmes et que jamais nul n'en peut rien cognoistre ou appercevoir par ses habillements, ne aultrement."

I leave this unpleasantly frank statement in the original Old French, merely remarking that it means that Jeanne never menstruated. D'Aulon must have had plenty of opportunities for knowing this, in his position as steward of her household in the field. He guards himself from innuendo by saying that several women had told him. Jeanne's failing to become mature must have been the topic of amazed conversation among all the women of her neighbourhood, and no doubt she herself took it as a sign from God that she was to remain virgin. It is especially significant that she first heard her Voices when she was about thirteen years of age, at the very time that she should have begun to menstruate; and that at first they did not come regularly, but came at intervals, just as menstruation itself often begins. Some months later she was informed by the Voices that she was to remain virgin, and thereby would she save France, in accordance with a prophecy that a woman should ruin France, and a virgin should save it. Is it not probable that the idea of virginity must have been growing in her mind from the time when she first realized that she was not to be as other women? Probably the delusion as to the Voices first began as a sort of vicarious menstruation; probably it recurred when menstruation should have reappeared; we can put the idea of virginity into the jargon of psycho-analysis by saying that Jeanne had well-marked "repression of the sex-complex." The mighty forces which should have manifested themselves in normal menstruation manifested themselves in her furious religious zeal and her Voices. Repression of the sex-complex is like locking up a giant in a cellar; sooner or later he may destroy the whole house. He ended by driving Jeanne d'Arc to the stake. That was a nobler fate than befalls some girls, whom the same giant drives to the streets; nobler, because Jeanne the peasant was of essentially noble stock. Her mother was Isabel Romée—the "Romed woman"—the woman who had had sufficient religious fervour to make the long and dangerous pilgrimage to Rome that she might acquire the merit of seeing the Holy Father; Jeanne herself made a still more dangerous pilgrimage, which has won for her the love of mankind at the cost of her bodily anguish. Madame her mother saved her own soul by her pilgrimage, and bore an heroic daughter; Jeanne saved France by her courage and devotion to her idea of God. And this would have been impossible had she not suffered from repression of the sex-complex and seen visions therefore.

Another remarkable piece of evidence has been omitted from the English translation. It was given by the Demoiselle Marguerite la Thoroulde, who had taken Jeanne to the baths and seen her unclothed. Madame la Thoroulde said, in the Latin translation of the Rehabilitation Trial which has survived: "Quod cum pluries vidit in balneo et stuphis [sweating-bath] et, ut percipere potuit, credit ipse fore virginem."

That is to say, she saw her naked in the baths and could see that she was a virgin! What on earth did the good lady think that a virgin would look like? Did she think that because Jeanne did not look like a stout French matron she must therefore be a virgin? Or did she see a strong and boyish form, with little development of hips and bust, which she thought must be nothing else but that of a virgin? That is the explanation that occurs to me; and probably it also explains Jeanne's idea that by wearing men's clothes she would render herself less attractive to the mediæval soldiery among whom her lot was to be cast. An ordinary buxom young woman would certainly not be less attractive because she displayed her figure in doublet and hose; Rosalind is none the less winsome when she acts the boy; and I should have thought that Jeanne, by wearing men's clothes, would simply have proclaimed to her male companions that she was a very woman. But if the idea be correct that she was shaped like a boy, with little feminine development, the whole mystery is at once solved. It is to be remembered that we know absolutely nothing about Jeanne's appearance[4]; the only credible hint we have is that she had a gentle voice.

In the Rehabilitation Trial several of her companions in arms swore that she had had no sexual attraction for them. It is quaint to read the evidence of these respectable middle-aged gentlemen that in their hot and lusty youth they had once upon a time met at least one young girl after whom they had not lusted; they seem to consider that the fact proved that she must have come from God. Anatole France makes great play with them, but it would appear that his ingenuity is in this direction misplaced. Is it not possible that Jeanne was unattractive to men because she was immature—that she never became more than a child in mind and body? Even mediæval soldiery would not lust after a child, especially a child whom they firmly believed to have come straight from God! It must be remembered that to half of her world

Jeanne was unspeakably sacred; to the other half she was undeniably a most frightful witch. Even the executioner would not imperil his immortal soul by touching her. It was the custom to spare a woman the anguish of the fire, by smothering her, or rendering her unconscious by suddenly compressing her carotids with a rope before the flames leaped around her. But Jeanne was far too wicked for anybody to touch in this merciful office; they had to let her die unaided; and afterwards, so wicked was her heart, they had to rescue it from the ashes and throw it into the Seine. Is it conceivable that men who thought thus would have ventured hell-fire by making love to her? Yet more—it is quite possible that she had no bodily charms whatever; we know nothing of her appearance. The story that she was charming and beautiful is simply sentimental legend. Indeed, it is difficult not to become sentimental over Jeanne d'Arc.

A noteworthy feature in her character was her Puritanism. She prohibited her soldiers from consorting with the prostitutes that followed the army; sometimes she even forced them to marry these women. Naturally the soldiers objected most strongly, and in the end this was one of the causes that led to her downfall. Jeanne used to run after the prohibited girls and strike them with the flat of her sword; in one case the girl was killed. In another the sword broke, and King Charles asked, very sensibly, "Would not a stick have done quite as well?" This is believed by some people to have been the very sword of Charles Martel which the priests had found for her at St. Catherine's command, and naturally the soldiers, deprived of their female companions, wondered what sort of a holy sword could it have been which could not even stand the smiting of a prostitute? When people suffer from repression of the sex-complex the trouble may show itself either by constant indirect attempts to find favour in the eyes of individuals of the opposite sex, or sometimes by actually forbidding all sexual matters; Puritanism in sexual affairs is often an indication that all is not quite well with a woman's subconscious mind; nor can one confine this generalization to one sex. It is not for one moment to be thought that Jeanne ever had the slightest idea of what was the matter with her; the whole of her delusions and Puritanism were to her quite conscious and real; the only thing that she did not know was that her delusions were entirely subjective—that her Voices had no existence outside her own mind. Her frantic belief in them led her to an heroic career and to the stake. She did not consciously repress her sex; Nature did that for her.

Women who never menstruate are not uncommon; most gynæcologists see a few. Though they are sometimes normal in their sexual feelings— sometimes indeed they are even nymphomaniacs or very nearly so—yet they seldom marry, for they know themselves to be sterile, and, after all, most women seem to know at the bottom of their hearts that the purpose of women is to produce children.

But there is still more of psychological interest to be gained from a careful reading of the first trial. It is possible to see how Jeanne's unstable nervous system reacted to the long agony. We had better, in order to be fair, make quite certain why she was burned. These are the words uttered by the good Bishop of Beauvais as he sentenced her for the last time:—

"Thou hast been on the subject of thy pretended divine revelations and apparitions lying, seducing, pernicious, presumptuous, lightly believing, rash, superstitious, a divineress and blasphemer towards God and the Saints, a despiser of God Himself in His sacraments; a prevaricator of the Divine Law, of sacred doctrine and of ecclesiastical sanctions; seditious, cruel, apostate, schismatic, erring on many points of our Faith, and by these means rashly guilty towards God and Holy Church."

This appalling fulmination, summed up, appears to mean—if it means anything—that she believed that she was under the direct command of God to wear man's clothes. To this she could only answer that what she had done she had done by His direct orders.

Theologians have said that her answers at the trial were so clever that they must have been directly inspired; but it is difficult to see any sign of such cleverness. To me her character stands out absolutely clearly defined from the very beginning of the six weeks' agony; she is a very simple, direct, and superstitious child struggling vainly in the meshes of a net spread for her by ecclesiastical politicians who were determined to sacrifice her to serve the ends of brutal masters. She had all a child's simple cunning; when the Bishop asked her to repeat her Paternoster she answered that she would gladly do so if he himself would confess her. She thought that if he confessed her he might have pity on her, or, at least, that he would be bound to send her to Heaven, because she knew how great was the influence wielded by a Bishop; she thought that she might tempt him to hear her in the secrets of the confessional if she promised to repeat her Paternoster to him! Poor child—she little knew what was at the bottom of the trial.

She sometimes childishly boasted. When she was asked if she could sew, she answered that she feared no woman in Rouen at the sewing; just so might answer any immature girl of her years to-day. She sometimes childishly threatened; she told the Bishop that he was running a great risk in charging her. She had delusions of sight, smell, touch, and hearing. She said that the faces of Saints Catherine and Margaret were adorned with beautiful crowns, very rich and precious, that the saints smelled with a sweet savour, that she had kissed them, that they spoke to her.

There was a touch of epigram about the girl, too. In speaking of her banner at Rheims, she said: "It had been through the hardships—it were well that it should share the glory." And again, when the judges asked her to what she attributed her success, she answered, "I said to my followers: 'Go ye in boldly against the English,' *and I went myself."* The girl who said that could hardly have been a mere military *mascotte.* Yet, in admitting so much, one does not admit that she may have been a sort of Amazon. As the desperation of her position grew upon her she began to suffer more and more from her delusions; while she lay in her dungeon waiting for the fatal cart she told a young friar, Brother Martin Ladvenu, that her spirits came to her in great numbers and of the smallest size. When despair finally seized upon her she told "the venerable and discreet Maître Pierre Maurice, Professor of Theology," that the angels really had appeared to her—good or bad, they really had appeared—in the form of very minute things[5]; that she now knew that they had deceived her. Her brain wearied by her long trial of strength with the Bishop, common sense re-asserted its sway, and she realized—the truth! Too late! When she was listening to her sermon on the scaffold in front of the fuel destined to consume her, she broke down and knelt at the preacher's knees, weeping and praying until the English soldiers called out to ask if she meant to keep them there for their dinner; it is pleasing to know that one of them broke his lance into two pieces, which he tied into the form of a cross and held it up to her in the smoke that was already beginning to arise about her.

Her last thoughts we can never know; her last word was the blessed name of Jesus, which she repeated several times. In public—though she had told Pierre Maurice in private that she had "learned to know that her spirits had deceived her"—she always maintained that she had both seen and believed them because they came from God; her courage was amazing, both physical and moral. She was twice wounded, but she said that she always carried her standard so that she would never have to kill anybody—and that in truth she had never killed anybody.

Her extraordinary accomplishment was due to the unbounded superstition of the French common people, who at first believed in her implicitly; it was Napoleon, a French general, who said that in war the moral is to the spiritual as three is to one; our Lord said, "By faith ye shall move mountains"; and it must not be forgotten that she went to Orleans with powerful reinforcements which she herself estimated at about ten to twelve thousand men. This superstition of the French was more than equalled by the superstition of the English, who looked upon her as a most terrifying witch: one witness at the Rehabilitation Trial said that the English were a very superstitious nation, so they must have been pretty bad. Indeed, most of the witnesses at that trial seem to have been very superstitious; one must examine their evidence with care lest one suddenly finds that one is assisting at a miracle.

She seems to have been hot-tempered and emphatic in her speech, with a certain tang of rough humour such as would be natural in a peasant girl. A notary once questioned the truth of something she said at her trial; on inquiry it was found that she had been perfectly accurate; Jeanne "rejoiced, saying to Boisguillaume that if he made mistakes again she would pull his ears." Once during the trial she was taken ill with vomiting, apparently caused by fish-poisoning, that followed after she had eaten of some carp sent her by the Bishop. Maître d'Estivet, the promoter of the trial, said to her, 'Thou *paillarde!*' (an abusive term), 'thou hast been eating sprats and other unwholesomeness!' She answered that she had not; and then she and d'Estivet exchanged many abusive words. The two doctors of medicine who treated her for this illness gave evidence, and it is pleasing to see that they seem to have been able to rationalize a trifle more about her than most of her contemporaries. But, taken all through, her evidence gives the impression of being exceedingly simple and straightforward—just the sort of thing to be expected from a child.

It is noteworthy that a great many witnesses at the Rehabilitation Trial swore that she was "simple." Did they mean that she was half-witted? Probably not. More probably it was true that she always wanted to spare her enemies, when, in accordance with the custom of the Hundred Years' War, she should rather have held them for ransom if they had been noble or slain them if they had been poor men. To the ordinary brutal mediæval soldiery such conduct would appear insane. Possibly, of course, the term "simple" might have been used in opposition to the term "gentle."

May I be allowed to give a vignette of Jeanne going to the burning, compiled from the evidence of many onlookers given at the Rehabilitation Trial? She assumed no martyresque imperturbability; she did not hold her head high in the haughty belief that she was right and the rest of the world wrong, as a martyr should properly do. She wept bitterly as she walked to the fatal cart from the prison-doors; her head was shaven; she wore woman's dress; her face was swollen and distorted, her eyes ran tears, her sobs shook her body, her wails moved the hearts of the onlookers. The French wept for sympathy, the English laughed for joy. It was a very human child who went to her death on May 30th, 1431. She was nineteen years of age—according to some accounts, twenty-one—and, unknown to herself, she had changed the face of history.

The Empress Theodora

THIS famous woman has been the subject of one of the bitterest controversies in history; and, while it is impossible to speak fully about her, it is certain that she was a woman of remarkable beauty, character, and historical position. For nearly a thousand years after her death she was looked upon as an ordinary—if unusually able—Byzantine princess, wife of Justinian the lawgiver, who was one of the ablest of the later Roman Emperors; but in 1623 the manuscript was discovered in the Vatican of a secret history, purporting to have been written by Procopius, which threw a new and amazing light on her career.

Procopius—or whoever wrote this most scurrilous history—states that the great Empress in early youth was an actress, daughter of a bear-keeper, and that she had sold tickets in the theatre; her youth had been disgustingly profligate: he narrates a series of stories concerning her which cannot be printed in modern English. The worst of these go to show that she was an ordinary type of Oriental prostitute, to whom the word "unnatural," as applied to vice, had no meaning. The least discreditable is that the girl who was to be Empress had danced nearly naked on the stage—she is not the only girl who has done this, and not on the stage either. She had not even the distinction of being a good dancer, but acquired fame through the wild abandon and indecency with which she performed. At about the age of twenty she married—when she had already had a son—the grave and stately Justinian: "the man who had never been young," who was so great and learned that it was well known that he could be seen of nights walking about the streets carrying his head in a tray like John the Baptist. When he fell a victim to Theodora's wiles he was about forty years of age. The marriage was bitterly opposed by his mother and aunts, but they are said to have relented when they met her, and even had a special law passed to legalize the marriage of the heir to the throne with a woman of ignoble birth; and, after the death of Justin, Theodora duly succeeded to the leadership of the proudest court in Europe. This may be true; but it does not sound like the actions of a mother and old aunts. One would have thought that a convenient bowstring or sack in the Bosphorus would have been the more usual course.

So far we have nothing to go by but the statements of one man; the greatest historian of his time, to be sure—if we can be certain that he wrote the book. Von Ranke, himself a very great critical historian, says flatly that Procopius never wrote it; that it is simply a collection of dirty stories current about other women long afterwards. The Roman Empire seems to have been a great hotbed for filthy tales about the Imperial despots: one has only to remember Suetonius, from whose lively pages most of our doubtless erroneous views concerning the Palatine "goings on" are derived; and to recall the foul stories told about Julius Cæsar himself, who was probably no worse than the average young officer of his time; and of the last years of Tiberius, who was probably a great deal better than the average. Those of us who can cast their memories back for a few years can doubtless recall an instance of scurrilous libel upon a great personage of the British Empire, which cast discredit not on the gentleman libelled but upon the rascal who spread the libel abroad. It is one of the penalties of Empire that the wearer of the Imperial crown must always be the subject of libels against which he has no protection but in the loyal friendship of his subjects. Even Queen Victoria was once called "Mrs. Melbourne," though probably even the fanatic who howled it did not believe that there was any truth in his insinuation. And Procopius did not have the courage to publish his libels, but preferred to leave to posterity the task of finding out how dirty was Procopius' mind. Probably he would not have lived very long had Theodora discovered what he really thought of her. He was wise in his generation, and had ever the example of blind Belisarius before him to teach him to walk cautiously.

Démidour in 1887, Mallet in 1889, and Bury also in 1889, have once more reviewed the evidence. The two first-mentioned go very fully into it, and sum up gallantly in Theodora's favour; but Bury is not so sure. Gibbon, having duly warned us of Procopius' malignity, proceeds slyly to tell some of the most printable of the indecent stories. Gibbon is seldom very far wrong in his judgments, and evidently had very little doubt in his own mind about Theodora's guilt. Joseph Maccabe goes over it all again, and "regretfully" believes everything bad about her. Edward Foord says, in effect, that supposing the stories were all true, which he does not appear to believe, and that she had thrown her cap over the windmills when she was a girl—well, she more than made up for it all when she became Empress. After all, it depends upon how far we can believe Procopius; and that again depends upon how far we can bring ourselves to believe that an exceedingly pretty little Empress can once upon a time have been a *fille de joie*. That in its turn depends upon how far each individual man is susceptible to female beauty. If she had been a prostitute it makes her career as Empress almost miraculous; it is the most extraordinary instance on record of "living a thing down," and speaks volumes for her charm and strength of personality.

She lived in the midst of most furious theological strife. Christianity was still a comparatively new religion, even if we accept the traditional chronology of the early world; and in her time the experts had not yet settled what were its tenets. The only thing that was perfectly clear to each theological expert was that if you did not agree with his own particular belief you were eternally damned, and that it was his duty to put you out of your sin immediately by cutting your throat lest you should inveigle some other foolish fellows into the broad path that leadeth to destruction. Theodora was a Monophysite—that is to say, she believed that Christ had only one soul, whereas it was well known to the experts that He had two. Nothing could be too dreadful for the miscreants who believed otherwise. It was gleefully narrated how Nestorius, who had started the abominable doctrine of Monophysm, had his tongue eaten by worms—that is, died of cancer of the tongue; and it is not incredible that Procopius, who was a Synodist or Orthodox believer, may have invented the libels and secretly written them down in order to show the world of after days what sort of monster his heretical Empress really was, wear she never so many gorgeous ropes of pearls in her Imperial panoply. It is difficult to place any bounds to theological hatred—or to human credulity for that matter. The whole question of the nature of Christ was settled by the Sixth Œcumenical Council about a hundred and fifty years later, when it was finally decided that Christ had two natures, or souls, or wills—however we interpret the Greek word Φύσις—each separate and indivisible in one body. This, and the Holy Trinity, are still, I understand, part of Christian theology, and appear to be equally comprehensible to the ordinary scientific man.

But it is difficult to get over a tradition of the eleventh century—that is to say, six hundred years before Procopius' *Annals* saw the light—that Justinian married "Theodora of the Brothel." Although Mallet showed that Procopius had strong personal reasons for libelling his Empress, one cannot help feeling that there must be something in the stories after all.

Once she had assumed the marvellous crown, with its ropes of pearls, in which she and many of the other Empresses are depicted, her whole character is said to have changed. Though her enemies accused her of cruelty, greed, treachery, and dishonesty—and no accounts from her friends have survived—yet they were forced to admit that she acted with propriety and amazing courage; and no word was spoken against her virtue. In the Nika riots, which at one time threatened to depose Justinian, she saved the Empire. Justinian, his ministers, and even the hero Belisarius, were for flight, the mob howling in the square outside the Palace, when Theodora spoke up in gallant words which I paraphrase. She began by saying how indecorous it was for a woman to interfere in matters of State, and then went on to say:

"We must all die some time, but it is a terrible thing to have been an Emperor and to give up Empire before one dies. The purple is a noble winding-sheet! Flight is easy, my Emperor—there are the steps of the quay—there are the ships waiting for you; you have money to live on. But in very shame you will taste the bitterness of death in life if you flee! I, your wife, will not flee, but will stay behind without you, and will die an Empress rather than live a coward!" Proud little woman—could that woman have been a prostitute selling her body in degradation? It seems impossible.

The Council, regaining courage, decided for fighting; armed bands were sent forth into the square; the riot was suppressed with Oriental ferocity; and the Roman Empire lasted nearly a thousand years more. "Toujours l'audace," as Danton said nearly thirteen hundred years later, when, however, he was not in imminent peril himself.

In person Theodora was small, slender, graceful, and exquisitely beautiful; her complexion was pale, her eyes singularly expressive: the mosaic at Ravenna, in stiff and formal art, gives some evidence of character and beauty. She was accused, as I have said, of barbarous cruelties, of herself applying the torture in her underground private prisons; the stories are contradictory and inconsistent, but one story appears to be historical: "If you do not obey me I swear by the living God that I will have you flayed alive," she said with gentle grace to her attendants. It is said that her illegitimate son, whom she had disposed of by putting him with his terrified father in Arabia, gained possession of the secret of his birth, and boldly repaired to Constantinople in the belief that her maternal affection would lead her to pardon him for the offence of having been born, and that thereby he would attain to riches and greatness; but the story goes that he was never seen again after he entered the Palace. Possibly the story is of the nature of romance. She dearly longed for a legitimate son, and the faithful united in prayer to that end; but the sole fruit of her marriage was a daughter, and even this girl was said to have been conceived before the wedding.

When she was still adolescent she went for a tour in the Levant with a wealthy Tyrian named Ecebolus, who, disgusted by her violent temper or her universal *charity*, to use Gibbon's sly phrase, deserted her and left her penniless at Alexandria. The men of Egypt appear to have been less erotic than the Greeks, for she remained in dire poverty, working her way back home by way of the shores of the Euxine. In Egypt she had become a Monophysite; and when she reached Constantinople it is said that she sat in a pleasant home outside the Palace and plied her spinning-wheel so virtuously that Justinian fell in love with her and ultimately married her, having first tried her charms. Passing over the obvious difficulty that a girl of the charm and immorality of Procopius' Theodora need never have gone in poverty while men were men, the wonder naturally arises whether the girl who went away with Ecebolus was the same as she who returned poor and alone and sat so virtuously at her spinning-wheel as to bewitch Justinian. Mistaken identity, or rather loss of identity, must have been commoner in those days than these when the printing-press and rapid postal and telegraphic communication make it harder to lose one's self. However, granting that there was no confusion of identity, one may believe—if one tries hard enough—that she was befriended by the Monophysites in Egypt, and may have "found religion" at their hands, and, by suffering poverty and oppression with them, had learned to sympathize with the under-world. Though the story may seem to be more suitable for an American picture-show than for sober history, still one must admit that it is not absolutely impossible. When she became great and famous she did not forget those who had rescued her in the days of her affliction; and her influence on Justinian is to be seen in the "feminism" which is so marked in his code. What makes it not impossible is the well-known fact that violent sexuality is in some way related to powerful religious instincts; and the theory that the passions which had led Theodora to the brothel may, when her mind was turned to religion, have led her to be a Puritan, is rather attractive. But nothing is said about Theodora which has not in some way been twisted to her infamy. The only certain fact about her is that she had enormous influence over her husband, and it is difficult to believe that a great and able man like Justinian could have entirely yielded his will to the will of a cruel and treacherous harlot. The idea certainly opens an unexpectedly wide vista of masculine weakness.

She used this influence in helping to frame the great Code of Justinian, which has remained the standard of law in many countries ever since. A remarkable feature about this code is that, while it is severe on the keepers of brothels, it is mild to leniency on the unhappy women who prostituted themselves for these keepers' benefit. The idea that a prostitute is a woman, with rights and feelings like any other woman, appears to have been unknown until Theodora had it introduced into the code of laws which perpetuates her husband's memory. One night she collected all the prostitutes in Constantinople, five hundred in all—were there only five hundred in that vast Oriental city?—shut them up in a palace on the Asiatic shore of the Bosphorus, and expected them to reform as she had reformed, but with less success; as our modern experience would lead us to expect. The girls grew morbidly unhappy, and many threw themselves into the sea. Even in a lock hospital we know how difficult it is to reclaim girls to whom sexual intercourse has become a matter of daily habit, and if Theodora's well-meant attempt failed we must at least give her credit for an attempt at an idealistic impossibility. These girls did not have the prospect of marrying an Emperor; no pearl-stringed crown was dangled before their fingers for the grasping. Poor human nature is not so easily kept on the strait and narrow path as Theodora thought. Throughout her life she seems to have had great sympathy for the poor and the oppressed, and one feels with Edward Foord that one can forgive her a great deal. We must not forget that her husband called her his "honoured wife," his "gift from God," and his "sweet delight"; and spoke most gratefully of her interest and assistance in framing his great code of laws. Was her humanitarianism, her sympathy with down-trodden women, the result of her own sad past experience? To think so would be to turn her pity towards vice into an argument against her own virtue, and I shrink from doing so. Let us rather believe that she really did perceive how terribly the Fates have loaded the dice against women, and that she did what she could to make their paths easier through this earth on which we have no continuing city.

Her health gave her a great deal of trouble, and she spent many months of every year in her beautiful villas on the shores of the Sea of Marmora and the Bosphorus. She remained in bed most of every day, rising late, and retiring early. To Procopius and the Synodists these habits were naturally signs of Oriental weakness and luxury; but may not the poor lady have been really ill? She visited several famous baths in search of health, and we have a vivid account of her journey through Bithynia on her way to the hot springs of the Pythian Apollo near Brusa.

We have no evidence as to the nature of her illness. Her early life, of course, suggests some venereal trouble, and it is interesting to inquire into the position of the various venereal diseases at that time. Syphilis I think we may rule out of court; for it is now generally believed that that disease was not known in Europe until after the return of Columbus' men from the West Indian islands. Some of the bones of Egypt were thought to show signs of syphilitic invasion until it was shown by Elliott Smith that similar markings are caused by insects; and no indubitable syphilitic lesion has ever been found in any of the mummies. If syphilis did really occur in European antiquity, it must have been exceedingly rare and have differed widely in its pathological effects from the disease which is so common and destructive to-day; that is to say, in spite of certain German enthusiasts, it could not have been syphilis.

But gonorrhœa is a very old story, and was undoubtedly prevalent in the ancient world. Luys indeed says that gonorrhœa is as old as mankind, and was named by Galen himself, though regular physicians and surgeons scorned to treat it. It is strange that there is so little reference to this disease in the vast amount of pornographic literature which has come down to us.

Martial, for instance, or Ovid; nothing would seem too obscene to have passed by their salacious minds; yet neither of them so much as hint that such a thing as gonorrhœa existed. But it is possible that such a disease might have been among the things unlucky or "tabu." All nations and all ages have been more or less under the influence of tabu, which ranges from influence on the most trivial matters to settlement of the gravest. Thus, many men would almost rather die than walk abroad in a frock coat and tan boots, or, still more dreadful, in a frock coat and Homburg hat, though that freakish costume appears to be common enough in America. In this matter we are under the influence of tabu—the thing which prevents us, or should prevent us, from eating peas with our knife, or making unseemly noises when we eat soup, or playing a funeral march at a cheerful social gathering. In all these things the idea of *nefas*—unlucky—seems more or less to enter; similarly we do not like to walk under a ladder lest a paint-pot should fall upon us. Many people hate to mention the dread word "death," lest that should untimely be their portion. Just so possibly a licentious man like Ovid may have been swayed by some such fear, and he may have refrained from writing about the horrid disease which he must have known was ever waiting for him.

But though it may seem to have been impossible that any prostitute should have escaped gonorrhœa in Byzantium, just as it is impossible in modern London or Sydney, yet there is no evidence that Theodora so suffered; what hints we have, if they weigh on either side at all, seem to make it unlikely. She had a child after her marriage with Justinian, though women who have had untreated gonorrhœa are very frequently or generally sterile. Nor is there any evidence that Justinian ever had any serious illness except the bubonic plague, from which he suffered, and recovered, during the great epidemic of 546. I assume that the buboes from which he doubtless suffered at that time were not venereal but were the ordinary buboes of plague. He had been Theodora's husband for many years before that terrible year in which the plague swept away about a third of the population of the Roman Empire, where it had been simmering ever since the time of Marcus Aurelius. If Theodora really had gonorrhœa, Justinian must have caught it, and it is unlikely that he would have called her his "honoured wife."

A more probable explanation of her continued ill-health might be that she became septic at her confinement, when the unwanted girl was born. When the Byzantines spoke of a child as being "born in the purple," they spoke literally, for the Roman Empress was always sent to a "porphyry palace" on the Bosphorus for her confinement; and once there she had access to less good treatment than is available for any sempstress to-day. It is impossible to suppose that the porphyry palace—the "purple house"—ever became infected with puerperal sepsis because there was never more than one confinement going on at a time within its walls, and that only at long intervals. Still, there must have been a great many septic confinements and unrecorded female misery from their results among the women of that early world; and that must be remembered when we consider the extraordinarily small birth-rate of the Imperial families during so many centuries. Had the Roman Emperors been able to point to strong sons to inherit their glories, possibly the history of the Empire would have been less turbulent. A Greek or Roman Lister might have altered the history of the world by giving security of succession to the Imperial despot.

After all, it is idle to speculate on Theodora's illness, and it does not much matter. She has long gone to her account, poor fascinating creature; all her beauty and wit and eager vivacity are as though they had never been save for their influence upon her husband's laws. Theodora is the standing example of woman's fate to achieve results through the agency of some man.

She died of cancer, and died young. There is no record of the original site of the cancer; the ecclesiastic who records the glad tidings merely relates joyfully that it was diffused throughout her body, as was only right and proper in one who differed from him in religious opinions. It is generally thought that it started in the breast. No doubt this is a modern guess, though of course cancer of the breast is notorious for the way in which its secondary growths spread through liver, lungs, bones, neck, spine, and so forth; and there is little reason to suppose that the guess is incorrect. After trying all the usual remedies for "lumps," her physicians determined to send her to the baths of Brusa, famous in miraculous cure. There were two large iron and two large sulphur springs, besides smaller ones; and people generally went there in spring and early summer when the earth was gaily carpeted with the myriad flowers that spring up and fade before the heat of the Mediterranean July. May we infer from the choice of a sulphur bath that the cancer had already invaded the skin? Possibly. Such a horror may have been the determining factor which induced the Empress and her physicians to travel afield. But if so, surely the recording priest missed a chance of rejoicing; for he does not tell us the glad news. All over Bithynia and the Troad there were, and are, hot mineral springs; Homer relates how one hot spring and a cold gushed from beneath the walls of Troy itself. The girls of Troy used to wash their clothes in the hot spring whenever Agamemnon would let them.

When Theodora went to Brusa she was accompanied by a retinue of four thousand, and Heaven resounded with the prayers of the Monophysites; but the Orthodox refused to pray for the recovery of so infamous a heretic, just as they had refused to join in her prayers for a son. Theodora met with little loving-kindness on this earth after she had left Egypt; possibly the world repaid her with what it received from her.

The sanctuaries of Asklepios were the great centres of Greek and Roman healing, and the treatment there was both mental and physical. The temples were generally built in charming localities, where everything was peace and loveliness; the patients lay in beds in beautiful colonnades, and to them, last thing at night, priests delivered restful and touching services; when sleep came upon them they dreamt, and the dreams were looked upon as the voice of God; they followed His instructions and were cured. They were not cured, however, if they had cancer. One Ælius Aristides has left us a vivid—and unconsciously amusing—account of his adventures in search of health; he seems to have been a neurotic man who ultimately developed into a first-class neurasthenic. To him his beloved god was indeed a trial, as no doubt Aristides himself was to his more earthly physicians. He would sit surrounded by his friends, to whom he would pour out his woes in true neurasthenic style. Aristides seems never to have been truly happy unless he was talking about his ailments, and he loyally followed any suggestion for treatment if only he could persuade himself that it came from the beloved Asklepios. The god would send him a vision, that ordered him to bathe three times in icy water when fevered, and afterwards to run a mile in the teeth of a north-east wind—and the north-easters in the Troad can be bitter indeed; very different from the urbane and gentle breath that spreads so delicious a languor over the summer of Sydney! This behest the much-tried man of faith would dutifully perform, accompanied by a running bodyguard of doctors and nurses marvelling at his endurance and the inscrutable wisdom of the god, though they expected, and no doubt in their inmost hearts hoped, that their long-suffering patient would drop dead from exhaustion. There were real doctors at these shrines besides priests. The doctors seem to have been much the same kind of inquisitive and benevolent persons as we are to-day; some of them were paid to attend the poor without fee. The nurses were both male and female, and appear to have been most immoral people. Aristides was the wonder of his age; his fame spread from land to land, and it is marvellous that he neither succumbed to his heroic treatment nor lost his faith in the divine being that subjected him to such torment. Both facts are perhaps characteristic of mankind. The manner of his end I do not know.

In Theodora's time Asklepios and the other Olympian divinities had long been gathered to their fathers before the advancing tides of Christianity and Earth-Mother worship; but though the old gods were gone the human body and human spirit remained the same, and there is no doubt that she was expected to dream and bathe and drink mineral waters just as Aristides had done centuries before; and no doubt a crowd of sympathizing friends sat round her on the marble seats which are still there and tried to console her—a difficult task when the sufferer has cancer of the breast. She sat there, her beauty faded, her once-rounded cheeks ashy with cachexia and lined with misery, brooding over the real nature of the Christ she was so soon to meet, wondering whether she or her implacable enemies were in the right as to His soul—whether He had in truth two souls or one. She had made her choice, and it was too late now to alter; in any case she was too gallant a little Empress to quail in the face of death, come he never so horribly. Let us hope that she had discovered before she died that Christ the All-merciful would forgive even so atrocious a sin as attributing to Him a single soul! All her piety, all the prayers of her friends, and all the medical skill of Brusa proved in vain, and she died in a.d. 548, being then forty years of age. So we take leave of this woman, whom many consider the most remarkable in history. Let us envisage her to ourselves—this graceful, exquisite, little cameo-faced lady, passionate in her loves and her hates, with some of the languor of the East in her blood, much of the tigress; brave in danger and resourceful in time of trouble; loyal and faithful to her learned husband as he was loyal to her; yet perhaps a little despising him. Except Medea, as seen by Euripides, Theodora was probably the first feminist, and as such has made her mark upon the world. On the whole her influence upon the Roman Empire seems to have been for good, and the merciful and juster trend of the laws she inspired must be noted in her favour.

Theodora dead, the glory of Justinian departed. He seemed to be stunned by the calamity, and for many critical months took no part in the world's affairs; even after he recovered he seemed but the shadow of his old self. Faithful to her in life, he remained faithful after her death, and sought no other woman; that is another reason for thinking that Procopius lied. He lived, a lonely and friendless old man, for eighteen more years, hated by his subjects for his extortionate taxation—which they attributed to the extravagance of the crowned prostitute, though more likely it was due to the enormous campaigns of Belisarius and Narses the eunuch, as a result of which Italy and Africa once more came under the sway of the East. Justinian was lonely on his death-bed, and the world breathed a sigh of relief when he was gone. He had long outlived his glory.

The Emperor Charles V

THAT extraordinary phenomenon which, being neither Holy, nor Roman, nor yet strictly speaking an Empire, was yet called the Holy Roman Empire, began when Charlemagne crossed the Alps to rescue the reigning Pope from the Lombards in a.d. 800. The Pope crowned him Roman Emperor of the West, a title which had been extinct since the time of Odoacer more than three hundred years before. The revival of the resplendent title caused the unhappy people of the Dark Ages to think for a moment in their misery that the mighty days of Augustus and Marcus Aurelius had returned; it seemed to add the power of God to the romance of ages and the brute power of kings. During the next two centuries the peoples of France and Germany gradually evolved into two separate nations, but it was impossible for men to forget the great brooding power which had given the *Pax Romana* to the world, and its hallowed memory survived more beneficent than possibly it really was; it appeared to their imaginations that if it were possible to unite the sanctity of the Pope with the organizing power of Rome the blessed times might again return when a man might reap in peace what he had sown in peace, and the long agony of the Dark Ages might be lifted from mankind. When Henry the Fowler had welded the Germans into a people with a powerful king the time appeared to have arisen, and his son Otto was crowned Holy Roman Emperor. He was not Emperor of Germany, nor German Emperor; he was *Holy Roman Emperor* of the German people, wielding power, partly derived from the religious power of the Pope, and partly from the military resources of whatever fiefs he might hold; and this enormous and loosely knit organization persisted until 1806—nearly seven hundred years from the time of Otto, and more than 1,000 years after the time of Charlemagne.

This mediæval Roman Empire was founded on sentiment; it took its power from blessed—and probably distorted—memories of a golden age, when one mighty Imperator really did rule the civilized world with a strong and autocratic hand. It was a pathetic attempt to put back the hands of the clock. It bespoke the misery through which mankind was passing in the attempt to combine feudalism with justice. When the mediæval Emperor was not fighting with the Pope he was generally fighting with his presumed subjects; occasionally he tried to defend Europe from the Turks. He might have justified his existence by defending Constantinople in 1453, by which he would have averted the greatest disaster that has ever befallen Europe. He missed that opportunity, and the mediæval Empire, though it survived that extraordinary calamity, yet continued ramshackle, feeble, and mediævally glorious until long past the Protestant Reformation. Being Roman, of course it was anti-Lutheran, and devoted its lumbering energies to the destruction of the Protestants. No Holy Roman Emperor ever rivalled the greatness of Charles V, in whose frame shone all the romance and glamour of centuries. How vast was his power is shown when we consider that he ruled over the Netherlands, Burgundy, Spain, Austria, much of what is now Germany, and Italy; and he was not a man to be contented with a nominal rule.

He was born in Ghent in 1500 to Philip, Duke of Burgundy, and Juana, who is commonly known as "Crazy Jane"; it is now generally believed that she was insane, though the Spaniards shrank from imputing insanity to a queen. From his father he inherited the principalities of the Netherlands and Burgundy; from his mother he inherited the kingships of Spain, Naples, and the Spanish colonies. When his grandfather, the Hapsburg Emperor Maximilian, died, Charles was elected Emperor in 1519; the other candidate was Francis I of France. The electors were the seven *Kurfursten* of Germany, and Charles bribed the harder of the two. What power on earth could summon before a magistrate the kings of France and Spain on a charge of improperly influencing the vote of a German princelet? Once having attained to the title of Roman Emperor, added to the enormous military power of King of Spain, Charles immediately became the greatest man in the world. He was strong, cautious, athletic, brave, and immeasurably sagacious; his reputation for wisdom long survived him.

Francis did not forgive him his victory, and for the next quarter of a century—until 1544—Europe resounded with the rival cries of the two monarchs, unhappy Italy being usually the actual scene of battle. At Pavia in 1525 Francis had to say "All is lost save honour" —the precise definition of "honour" in Francis's mind being something very different from what it is to-day. Francis was captured and haled to Madrid to meet his grim conqueror, who kept him in prison until he consented to marry Charles's favourite sister Eleanor of Austria, and to join with him in an alliance against the heretics. This Eleanor was a gentle and beautiful lady whom Charles treated with true brotherly contempt; yet she loved him. As soon as Francis was out of prison he forgot that he was married, and made love to every pretty girl that came his way.

Francis being safely out of the way, Charles turned to the great aim of his life—to reconcile Protestants with Catholics throughout his colossal Empire. He was a strong Catholic, and displayed immense energy in the reconciliation. According to Gibbon, who quotes the learned Grotius,[6] he burned 100,000 Netherlanders, and Gibbon dolefully remarks that this one Holy Roman Emperor slew more Christians than all the pagan Roman Emperors put together. Charles appears to have grown gradually into the habit of persecution; he began comparatively mildly, and it was not till 1550 that he began to see that there was really nothing else to do with these dull and obstinate Lutherans but to burn them. He could not understand it. He was sure he was right, and yet the more Netherlanders he burned the fewer seemed to attend mass. Moreover, it was impossible to believe that those things the miscreant Luther had said about the immoral conduct of the monks could be true; once upon a time he had met the fellow, and had him in his power; why had he not burned him once and for all and saved the world from this miserable holocaust which had now become necessary through the man's pestilential teaching? So Charles went on with his conciliation, driven by conscience—the most terrible spur that can be applied to the flanks of a righteous man. No doubt Torquemada acted from conscience, and Robespierre; possibly even Nero could have raked up some sort of a conscientious motive for all he did—the love of pure art, perhaps. "*Qualis artifex pereo!*" said he in one of those terse untranslatable Latin phrases when he was summoning up his courage to fall upon his sword in the high Roman manner; surely there spoke the artist: "How artistically I die!"

The activities of Charles were so enormous that it is impossible in this short sketch even to mention them all. Besides his conquest of Francis and, through him, Italy, he saved Europe from the Turk. To Francis's eternal dishonour he had made an alliance with the last great Turkish Sultan, Solyman the Magnificent. The baleful power which had conquered Constantinople less than a century before seemed to be sweeping on to spread its abominations over Western Europe; and history finds it difficult to forgive Francis for assisting its latest conqueror. Men remembered how Constantine Palæologus had fallen amidst smoke and carnage in his empurpled blazonry, heroic to the last; they forgot that the destruction of 1453 was probably the direct result of the Venetian and French attack under Dandolo in 1204, from which Constantinople never recovered. In talking of the "Terrible Turk" they forgot that Dandolo and his Venetians and Frenchmen had committed atrocities quite as terrible as the Turks' during those days and nights when Constantinople was given over to rapine; and now the brilliant Francis appeared to be carrying on Dandolo's war against civilization. So when Charles stepped forward as the great hero of Europe, and drove the Turks down the Danube with an army under his own leadership he was hailed as the saviour of Christendom; it is to this that he owes a good deal of his glory, and he nobly prepared the world for the still greater victory of Lepanto to be won by his son Don John of Austria.

Moreover, it was during his reign that the great American conquests of the Spanish armies occurred, and the name of Fernando Cortes attained to eternal glory; and the Portuguese voyager Maghellan made those wonderful discoveries which have so profoundly influenced the course of history. There had been no man so great and energetic as Charles since Charlemagne; since him his only rival for almost super-human energy has been Napoleon.

That pathetic and unhappy queen whom we call "Bloody Mary" had been betrothed to Charles for diplomatic reasons when she was an infant, but he had broken off the engagement and ultimately married Isabella of Portugal, whose fair face is immortalized by Titian in the portrait that still hangs in the Prado, Madrid. Auburn of hair, with blue eyes and delicate features, she looks the very type of what we used to call the tubercular diathesis; and there can be no doubt that Charles really loved her. Before he married her he had had an illegitimate daughter by a Flemish girl; ten years after she died Barbara Blomberg, a flighty German, bore him a son, the famous Don John of Austria. But while Isabella lived no scandal attached to his name. Unhappily his only legitimate son was Philip, afterwards Philip II of Spain.

When Mary came to the throne she was intensely unhappy. During the dreadful years that preceded the divorce of Catherine of Aragon, Charles had strongly supported Catherine's cause; and Mary did not forget his aid when she found herself a monarch, lonely and friendless. She let him know that she would be quite prepared to marry him if he would take her.[7] Probably Charles was terrified by the advances of the plain-faced old maid, but the opportunity of strengthening the Catholic cause was too good to miss. The house of Austria was always famous for its matrimonial skill; the hexameter pasquinade went:

"Bella gerant alii—tu, felix Austria, nube!"
("Others wage war for a throne—you, happy Austria, marry!")

Charles, in his dilemma, turned to his son Philip, who nobly responded to the call of duty. Of him Gibbon might have said that "he sighed as a lover, but obeyed as a son" if he had not said it concerning himself; and Philip broke off his engagement to the Infanta of Portugal, and married the fair English bride himself.

Charles was still the greatest and most romantic figure in Europe—a mighty conqueror and famous Emperor; any woman would have preferred him to his mean-spirited son; and Mary was grateful to him for powerful support during years of anguish. She obeyed his wishes, and took the son instead of the father.

Queen Mary's sad life deserves a word of sympathetic study. With her mother she had passed through years of hideous suffering, culminating in her being forced by her father to declare herself a bastard—probably the most utterly brutal act of Henry's reign. She had seen the fruits of ungovernable sexuality in the fate of her enemy Anne Boleyn; added to her plain face this probably caused her to repress her own sex-complex; finally she married the wretched young creature Philip, who, having stirred her sexual passions, left her to pursue his tortuous policy in Spain. All the time, as I read the story, she was really desirous of Charles, his brilliant father. Love-sick for Charles; love-sick for Philip, to whom she had a lawful right set at naught by leagues of sea; love-sick for *any* man whom her pride would allow her to possess—and I do not hint a word against her virtue—she is not a creature to scorn; she is rather to be pitied. Her father had been a man of strong passions and violent deeds; from him she had inherited that tendency to early degeneration of the cardiovascular system which led to her death from dropsy at the early age of forty-two; and her repressed sex-complex led her into the ways of a ruthless religious persecution, probably increased by the object-lesson set her by her hero. From this repressed sex-complex also sprang her fierce desire for a child, though the historians commonly attribute this emotion to a desire for some one to carry on her hatred of the Protestants. I remember the case of a young woman who was a violent Labour politician; unfortunately it became necessary for her to lose her uterus because of a fibroid tumour. She professed to be frantically sorry because she could no longer bear a son to go into Parliament to fight the battle of the proletariat against the wicked capitalist; but once in a moment of weakness she confessed that what she had really wanted was not a bouncing young politician, but merely a dear little baby to be her own child. Probably some such motive weighed with Mary. People laughed at her because she used to mistake any abdominal swelling, or even the normal diminution of menstruation that occurs with middle age, for a sign of pregnancy[8]; but possibly if she had married Charles instead of Philip, and had lived happily with him as his wife, she would not have given her people occasion to call her "Bloody Mary." She is the saddest figure in English history. From her earliest infancy she had been taught to look forward to a marriage with the wonderful man who to her mind—and to the world's—typified the noblest qualities of humanity—courage, bravery, rich and profound wisdom, learning and love of the beautiful in art and music and literature; friend and admirer of Titian and gallant helper of her mother. Her disappointment must have been terrible when she found him snatched from her grasp and saw herself condemned either to a life of old maidenhood or to a loveless marriage with a mean religious fanatic twelve years younger than herself. The mentality which led Mary to persecute the

English Protestants contained the same qualities as had led Joan of Arc to her career of unrivalled heroism, and to-day leads an old maid to keep parrots. When an old maid undresses it is said that she puts a cover over the parrot's cage lest the bird should see her nakedness; that is a phase of the same mentality as Mary's and Joan's. Loneliness, sadness, suppressed longing for the unattainable—it is cruel to laugh at an old maid.

But Charles was to show himself mortal. He had always been a colossal eater, and had never spared himself either in the field or at the table. One has to pay for these things; if a man wishes to be a great leader and to undertake great responsibilities he must be content to forswear carnal delights and eat sparingly; and it is hardly an exaggeration to say that it is less harmful to drink too much than to eat too much. At the age of thirty Charles began to suffer from "gout"—whatever it was that they called gout in those days. At the age of fifty he began to lose his teeth—apparently from pyorrhœa. Possibly his "gout" may have really been the result of focal infection from his septic teeth. At fifty his gout "flew to his head," and threatened him with sudden death. When he was fifty-two he suddenly became pale and thin, and it was noticed that his hair was rapidly turning grey. Clearly his enormous gluttony was beginning to result in arterio-sclerosis, and at fifty-four it was reported to his enemy the Sultan that Charles had lost the use of an arm and a leg. Sir William Stirling-Maxwell thought that this report was the exaggeration of an enemy; but it is quite possible that Charles really suffered from that annoying condition known as "intermittent claudication," which is such a nuisance to both patient and doctor in cases of arterio-sclerosis. In these attacks there may be temporary paralysis and loss of the power of speech. The cause of them is not quite clear, because they seldom prove fatal; but it is supposed that there is spasm of some small artery in the brain, or perhaps a transitory dropsy of some motor area. Charles's speech became indistinct, so that towards the end of his life it was difficult to understand what he meant. It has generally been supposed that this was due to his underhung lower jaw and loss of teeth; but it is equally probable that dropsy of the speech-centre may have been at the root of the trouble, such as is so frequently observed in arterio-sclerosis or its congener chronic Bright's disease, and is also often caused by over-strain and over-eating. He began to feel the cold intensely, and sat shivering even under the warmest wraps; he said himself that the cold seemed to be in his bones. Probably there was some spasm of the arterioles, such as is often seen in arterio-sclerosis.

By this time, what with the failure of his plans against the Protestants and his wretched health, he had made up his mind to resign the burden of Empire, and to seek repose in some warmer climate, where he could rest in the congenial atmosphere of a monastery. No Roman Emperor had voluntarily resigned the greatest position in the world since Diocletian in a.d. 305; curiously enough he too had been a persecutor, so that his reign is known among the hagiographers as "the age of martyrs."

Charles called together a great meeting at the Castle of Caudenburg in Brussels in 1556. All the great ones of the Empire were there, and the Knights of the Golden Fleece, an order which still vies for greatness with our own order of the Garter; possibly it may now even excel that order, because it is unlikely that it will ever again be conferred by an Austrian Emperor. Like the Garter, it had "no damned pretence of merit about it." If you were entitled to wear the chain and insignia of the Golden Fleece, you were a man of very noble birth. Yet, like the Order of the Thistle, the Fleece may yet be revived, and may recover its ancient splendour. On the right of the Emperor sat his son Philip, just returned, a not-impetuous bridegroom, from marrying Mary of England. On his left he leant painfully and short of breath upon the shoulder of William the Silent, who was soon to become of some little note in the world. It was a strange group: the great, bold Emperor whose course was so nearly run; the mean little king-consort of England; and the noble patriot statesman who was soon to drag Philip's name in the dust of ignominy. Charles spoke at some length, recounting how he had won many victories and suffered many defeats, yet, though so constantly at war, he had always striven for peace; how he had crossed the Mediterranean many times against the Turk, and had made forty long journeys and many short ones to see for himself the troubles of his subjects. He insisted proudly that he had never done any man a cruelty or an injustice. He burst into tears and sat down, showing the emotionalism that so often attends upon high blood-pressure; and the crowd, seeing the great soldier weep, wept with him. Eleanor gave him a cordial to drink, and he resumed, saying that at last he had found the trials of Empire more than his health would allow him to sustain. He had decided to abdicate in favour of his beloved son Philip. It was given to few monarchs to die and yet to live—to see his own glory continued in the glory which he expected for his son. It seems to have been a really touching and dramatic scene, causing an immense sensation throughout Europe. If there were ever an indispensable man it would have appeared at that time to be the Emperor Charles V; the world quaked in apprehension.

It was some time before Charles could carry out his design, but ultimately he went, by a long and dangerous journey, to the place of his retirement, Yuste, in Estremadura, Northern Spain, where there slept a little monastery of followers of St. Jerome; why he—a Fleming—should have picked on this lonely and inaccessible place is not known. With him went a little band of attendants, chief among whom was his stout old chamberlain, Don Luis Quixada, of whom we shall hear more when we come to consider Don John of Austria. This Quixada seems to have been a fine type of Spanish grandee, loyal and faithful; a merry grandee also, who added sound sense to jocund playfulness. Note well the name; we shall meet it again to some purpose.

Charles was mistaken in supposing that he could find rest at Yuste; the world would not let him rest. He had been a figure too overwhelming. He spent his days in reading dispatches from all who were in trouble and fancied that the great man could pluck them from the toils. Chief of his suppliants was his son Philip, who found the mantle that had seemed to sit so easily on his father's mighty shoulders intolerably heavy when he came to wear it himself. To the man who is strong in his wisdom and resolution difficulties disappear when they are boldly faced. Philip was timorous, poor-spirited, pedantic, and procrastinating. He constantly appealed to his father for advice, and Charles responded in letters which seem to show, in their evidence of annoyance, the irritability that goes with a high blood-pressure. An epidemic of Reformation was breaking out in Spain, however sterile might seem the soil of that nation for Protestantism to flourish. It is not quite clear why no serious move towards the Reformed Religion ever took place among the Spaniards. It is probable that the ancient faith had thrust its roots too deeply into their hearts during the centuries of struggle against the Moors. In the minds of the Spanish people it had been the Church which had inspired their ancestors—not the kings; and they were not going to desert the old religion now that they saw it attacked by the Germans. Moreover, the fierce repression which was practised by the Spanish Inquisition must have had its effect. Lecky formed the opinion that no new idea could survive in the teeth of really determined persecution; and the history of religion in Spain and France seems to bear him out.

However, the old war-horse in his retirement snuffed the battle and the joyous smell of the burnings, and stoutly urged on the Inquisitors, at whatever cost to his own quiet. Spain remained diligently Roman Catholic at the orders of the Holy Roman Emperor and his son Philip; and at this moment, when Charles was so urgently longing for peace and retirement, English Mary, his cousin and daughter-in-law, in whose interests he had loyally braved God, man, and Pope, lost Calais; the French, under the Duke of Guise, took it from her. She might well grieve and say the name would be found written on her heart; she but echoed the feelings of her beloved Emperor. For weeks he mumbled with toothless jaws the agony of his soul over this crowning misfortune, and from this he never really recovered. Already how had the times changed since the Spanish infantry had overrun Europe at his command!

But he could do nothing; he had abdicated. That iron hand was now so crippled with gout that it could hardly even open an envelope, had to sign its letters with a seal, and constantly held a tiny chafing-dish to keep itself warm. Charles sat shivering and helpless, wrapped in a great eiderdown cloak even in midsummer; his eyes fell on the portrait of his beloved wife and of that plain Mary who had wished to marry him, and on several favourite pictures by Titian. He listened to the singing of the friars, and was resentful of the slightest wrong note, for he had an exceedingly acute musical ear. The good fathers, in their attempts to entertain him, brought famous preachers to preach to him; he listened dutifully—he, whose lightest word had once shaken Europe, but who now could hardly mumble in a slurring voice! And in spite of the protests of Quixada he heroically sat down to eat himself to death. It has been said that marriage for an old man is merely a pleasant way of committing suicide; it is doubtful whether Charles enjoyed his chosen method of self-poisoning, for he had lost the sense of taste, and no food could be too richly seasoned for his tired palate. Vast quantities of beef, mutton, venison, ham, and highly flavoured sausages went past those toothless jaws, washed down by the richest wines, the heaviest beers; the local hidalgoes quickly discovered that to reach the Emperor's heart all they had to do was to appeal to his stomach, so they poured in upon him every kind of rich dainty, to the despair of Quixada, who did his best to protect his master. "Really," said he, "kings seem to think that their stomachs are not made like other men's!"

He sometimes used to go riding, but one day, when he was mounting his pony, he was suddenly seized with an attack of giddiness so severe that he nearly fell into the arms of Quixada, so that the Emperor, who had once upon a time been the *beau ideal* of a light cavalryman, had to toil about heavily on foot in the woods, and to strive to hold his gun steadily enough to shoot a wood-pigeon.

He spent his spare time watching men lay out for him new parterres and planting trees; man began with a garden, and in sickness and sorrow ends with one. The Earth-Mother is the one friend that never deserts us.

For some time he took a daily dose of senna, which was probably the best thing he could have taken in the absence of Epsom salts, but nothing could get rid of the enormous amount of rich food that poured down his gullet. He was always thinking of death, and there seems to be little doubt that he really did rehearse his own funeral. He held a great and solemn procession, catafalque and all, and, kneeling in front of the altar, handed to the officiating friar a taper, which was symbolical of his own soul. He then sat during the afternoon in the hot sun, and it was thought that he caught a feverish chill, for he took to his bed and never left it alive; for hours he held the portrait of Isabella in his hands, recalling her fresh young beauty; he clasped to his bosom the crucifix which he had taken from her dead fingers just before they had become stiff. Then came the fatal headache and vomiting which so often usher in the close of chronic Bright's disease. We are told that he lay unconscious, holding his wife's crucifix, till he said: "Lord, I am coming to Thee!" His hand relaxed—was the motor-centre becoming œdematous?—and a bishop held the crucifix before his dying eyes. Charles sighed, "Aye—Jesus!" and died. Whether or no he died so soon after saying these things as the good friar would have us believe, it is certain that his end was edifying and pious, and such as he would have wished.

The great interest of Charles V to a doctor, now that the questions over which he struggled so fiercely are settled, is that we can seldom trace so well in any historical character the course of the disease from which he died. If Charles had been content to live on milky food and drink less it is probable that he would have lived for years; he might have yielded to the constant entreaties of his friends and resumed the imperial crown; he might have taken into his strong hands the guidance of Spain and the Netherlands that was overwhelming Philip; his calm good sense might have averted the rising flood that ultimately led to the revolt of the Netherlands; possibly he might even have averted the Spanish Armada, though it seems improbable that he could have lived thirty years. But Spain might have avoided that arrogant behaviour which has since that day caused so many of her troubles; with the substitution of Philip for Charles at that critical time she took a wrong turning from which she has never since recovered.

The death of Charles V caused an extraordinary sensation in Europe— even greater than the sensation caused by his abdication. Immense memorial services were held all over the Empire; people wondered how they were ever to recover from the loss. Stout old Quixada said boldly that Charles V was the greatest man that ever had been or ever would be in the world. If we differ from him, at all events his opinion helps us to appreciate the extraordinary impression that Charles had made upon his time, and it is now generally agreed that he was the greatest man of the sixteenth century, which was so prodigal of remarkable men. Possibly William the Silent might be thought still greater; but he was much less resplendent; he lacked the knightly glamour that surrounded the head of the Holy Roman Emperor; he wore no Golden Fleece; no storied centuries fluttered over his head. Yet, if we come to seek a cause for this immense impression, it is not easy to find. There is no doubt that he was a stout defender of the old religion at a time when it sorely needed defenders, and to that extent Romance broods over his memory—the romance of things that are old. He was a man of remarkable energy, and a great soldier at a time when soldiering was not distinguished by genius. He appears to have had great personal charm, though I can find few sayings attributed to him by which we can judge the source of that charm. There is nothing in his history like the gay insouciance, the constant little personal letters to friends, of Henri Quatre; things with Charles V seem to have been rather serious and legal than friendly. He was fond of simple joys, like watchmaking, and he got a remarkable clockmaker, one Torriano, to accompany him to Yuste to amuse his last months. He left behind him a great many watches, and naturally the story grew that he had said: "If I cannot even get my watches to agree, how can I expect my subjects to follow one religion?" But it is probable that this pretty story is quite apocryphal; it is certainly very unlike Charles's strongly religious—not to say bigoted—character. He was proud and autocratic, yet could unbend, and the friars of Yuste found him a good friend. The boys of the neighbouring village used to rob his orchard, much to the disgust of the Emperor; he set the police on their track, but died before the case came up for trial. After his death it was found that he had left instructions that the fines which he expected to receive from the naughty little ragamuffins were to be given to the poor of their village. Among these naughty little boys was probably young Don John of Austria, whom Quixada had brought to see his supposed father; and it is said that Charles acknowledged him before he died.

Lastly, Charles had the inestimable advantage of being depicted by one of the greatest artists of all time. It is impossible to look upon his sad and thoughtful face, as drawn by the great Titian, without sympathy. The strong, if underhung, jaw which he bequeathed to his descendants and is still to be seen in King Alfonso of Spain; the wide-set and thoughtful eyes; the care-worn furrowed brow; the expression of energy and calm wisdom: all these belonged to a great man.

Two hundred years after he died, when his body had long been removed to the Escorial where it now lies in solemn company with the bodies of many other Spanish monarchs, a strange fate allowed a visiting Scotsman to view it. Even after that great lapse of time it was, though mummified, little affected by decay; there were still on his winding-sheet the sprigs of thyme which his friends had placed there; and the grave and stately features as painted by Titian were still vividly recognizable.

We should be quite within the bounds of reason in saying that Charles V was the greatest man between Charlemagne and Napoleon. He was less knightly than Charlemagne—probably because we know more about him; he had no Austerlitz nor Jena to his credit—nor any Moscow; but in devouring energy and vastness of conception there was little to choose between the three. Charlemagne left behind him the Holy Roman Empire with its enormous mediæval significance, whereas Napoleon and Charles V left comparatively little or nothing. He was the heroic defender of a losing cause, and wears the romantic halo that such heroes wear; yet whatever halo of chivalry, romance, and religious fervour surrounds his name, it is difficult to forget that he deliberately ate himself to death. An ignoble end.

Don John of Austria, Cervantes, and Don Quixote

TWO great alliances, of which you will read nothing in ordinary history-books, have pre-eminently influenced mankind. The first was between the Priest and the Woman, and seems to have begun in Neolithic times, when Woman was looked upon as a witch with some uncanny power of bewitching honest men and somehow bringing forth useless brats for no earthly reason that could be discovered. From this alliance grew the worship of Motherhood, and hence many more modern religions. When, on Sundays, you see ranks of men in stiff collars sitting in church though they would much rather be playing tennis, you know that they are expiating in misery the spankings inflicted by their Neolithic ancestors perhaps 10,000 years ago: their wives have driven them to church, and Woman, as usual, has had the last word.

But the other alliance, that between Man and Horse, has been a more terrible affair altogether, and has led to Chivalry, the cult of the Man on the Horse, of the Aristocrat, of the Rich Man. Though the Romans had a savage aristocracy they never had Chivalry, probably because they never feared the cavalryman. The Roman legion, in its open order, could face any cavalry, because the legionary knew that the man by his side would not run away; if he, being a misbegotten son of fear, did so, then the man behind him would take advantage of the plungings of the horse to drive his javelin into the silly animal while he himself would use his sword upon the rider. It was left for the Gran Catalan Company of Spain and the Scots under Wallace and Bruce to prove in mediæval times that the infantryman would beat the cavalryman.

The Romans never adopted the artificial rules of Chivalry; it was the business of the legions to win battles—to make money over the business if they could, but first and foremost to win battles. They had no ideas about the "point of honour" which has cost so many a man his life. The main thing was that the legions must not run away; it was for the enemy to do the running. To the Romans it never seems to have occurred that Woman was a creature to be sentimentally worshipped, or that it really mattered very much whether you spoke of a brace of grouse or a couple, of a mob of hounds or a pack; but to the Knight of Chivalry these were vital matters.

With Charlemagne and his Franks a new civilization came into full flower; and Chivalry—the "worship of God and the ladies," to quote Gibbon's ironic phrase—swayed the minds of Northern Europe for centuries.

Chivalry has been much misunderstood in modern times. We probably see Chaucer's "varry parfit gentil knight" as poets and idealists would have us see him and not as he really was. There was no sentimentality about your knight. "Gentle" did not mean "kind"; it meant really "son of a landowner." A knight had to do things in the manner considered fashionable by his class; he had to call things precisely by the names taught him by some older knight—his tutor and university combined; the slightest slip and he would be considered as the mediæval equivalent of our "bounder"; he had to wear the proper clothes at the proper time, and to obey certain arbitrary—often quite artificial—"manners and rules of good society," or he would be considered lacking in "good form"; he must recognize the rights of the rich as against the poor, but it did not follow that he should recognize any rights of the poor as against the rich. Even Bayard, knight *sans peur et sans reproche*, would probably have seemed a most offensive fellow to a twentieth-century gentleman if he, with his modern ideas, could have met the Chevalier; and the sensation caused by the kindly conduct of Sir Philip Sidney in handing his drink of water to a wounded soldier at Zutphen shows how rare such a thing must have been. It was done a thousand times in the late war, and nobody thought anything about it. To the extent of the sensation of Zutphen Chivalry had debased mankind; the evil that it did lived after it. It did good in teaching the world manners and a certain standard of honourable conduct; it did not teach morality, or real religion, or real kindness. These things were left for the poor to teach the rich.

This unsentimental harangue leads us to "the last knight of Europe"—Don John of Austria, around whose name there still shines a glamour of romance like the sound of a trumpet. About nine years after the death of the Empress Isabel, Charles V went a-wandering, still disconsolate, through his mighty empire. He was sad and lonely, for it was about the time when the arterio-sclerosis which was to kill him began to depress his spirits. At Ratisbon, where he lay preparing for the great campaign which was to end in the glorious victory of Muhlburg, they brought to him to cheer him up a sweet singer and pretty girl named Barbara Blomberg, daughter of a noble family. She sang to the Emperor to such purpose that he became her lover, and in due course Don John was born. By this time Charles had discovered that his pretty nightingale was a petulant, extravagant, sensual young woman, by no means the sort of mother a wise man would select to bring up his son; so he took the boy from her care and sent him to a poor Spanish family near Madrid. Whatever Charles V did in his private life seems to have borne the stamp of wisdom and kindness, however little we may agree with some of his public actions. Probably Barbara did not object; it must have been rather alarming for the flighty young person to have the tremendous personality of the great Emperor constantly overlooking her folly; she married a man named Kugel, ruined him by her extravagance, and died penniless save for an annuity of 200 florins left her by the Emperor in his will. I read a touch of sentimentality into Charles's character. It is difficult to wonder more at his memory of his old light-of-love in his will, or at his accurate and uncomplimentary estimate of her value. Probably he was rather ashamed of some of his memories; so far as I can find out there were not many such, and he wished to hush up the whole incident. Probably Barbara was not worth much more than 200 florins per annum.

Still keeping secret the parentage of the child, whom he called Jeronimo after his favourite saint, Charles handed him over to the care of his steward, Don Luis de Quixada, asking that Maddalena his wife should regard Jeronimo as her own son. Quixada had not been married very long, and naturally Maddalena wondered whence came this cheery little boy of which Quixada seemed so fond; nor would he gratify her curiosity, but hushed her with dark sayings; she kissed the baby in public, but wept in secret for jealousy of the wicked female who had evidently borne a son in secret to her husband before he had married his lawful wife. One night the castle caught fire, and Quixada, flower of Spain's chivalry though he was, rescued the child before he returned to save Maddalena. It is wrong to call him a "grandee of Spain," for "grandee" is a title much the same as our "duke"; had he been a grandee I understand that his true name would have been "Señor Don Quixada, duca e grandi de España." One would think that this action would have added fuel to Maddalena's jealousy, but she believed her husband when he told her that Jeronimo was a child of such surpassing importance to the world that it had been necessary for a Quixada to save him even before he saved his wife, and quite probably she then, for the first time, began to suspect his real parentage. Charles V was then the great Catholic hero, and the whole Catholic world was weeping for his abdication. So Maddalena developed a strong love for Jeronimo, which died only with herself. She lived for a great many years and bore no children; Jeronimo remained to her as her only son. He always looked upon her as his mother, and throughout his life wrote to her letters which are still delightful to read; whatever duty he had, in whatever part of the world, he always found time to write to Maddalena in the midst of it, and, like a real mother, she kept the letters.

It is said that Charles when dying kissed Jeronimo and called him son; he certainly provided for him in his will. After his death Quixada at first tried to keep the matter secret, but afterwards sent him to live at the Court with his brother Philip II, who treated him as he treated everybody else but Charles V — "the one wise and strong man whom he never suspected, never betrayed, and never undervalued," as Stirling-Maxwell says. Jeronimo was then openly acknowledged by Philip as Charles's natural son, being called Don John of Austria. Philip's own son, a youth of small intelligence, who afterwards died under restraint — Philip was of course accused of poisoning him — once called him *bâtarde et fils de putaine* — bastard and strumpet's son. The curly-headed little boy kept his hands by his side and quietly replied, "Possibly so; but at any rate I had a better *father* than you!" Even by that time he had begun to see that his mother was no saint, and could tell between a great man and a little. Philip could never forgive Don John for being a gallant youth such as his father had hoped that Philip would be and was not; and Don John, conscious of his mighty ancestry, ardently longed to be a real gallant King of Romance, such as his father had hoped Philip would become. Charles, in his will, had expressed a hope that he would be a monk, and Philip actively fought for this, though Charles had left the decision to Don John's own wishes. In Philip's eyes no doubt a gay and bold younger brother would be less dangerous to the State — i.e. to Philip — as a monk than as a soldier; yet is it not possible that Philip only thought he was loyally helping to follow out his father's wishes? He was generally a "slave of duty," though his slavery often led him into tortuous courses. The Church is a great leveller, and religion is a pacifying and amaranthine repast. But no monkish cowl would suit Don John; his locks were fair and hyacinthine, and no tonsure should degrade them. After a struggle Philip yielded, and Don John was sent in command of the galleys against the Algerian pirates. He did well, and next year he commanded the land forces against the rebel Moriscoes of Granada. Here, in his very first battle, he lost his foster-father and mentor, Quixada, who died a knightly death in rallying the army when it meditated flight. A true knight of Spain, this Quixada, from the time when he took the little son of imperial majesty under his care till the time when he gave up his life lest that little son, now become a radiant young man, should suffer dishonour by his army running away. All Spain, from Philip downward, mourned the death of this most valiant gentleman, which is another thing that makes me think that Philip's conduct towards Don John was not quite so black as it has been painted. He could certainly recognize worth when it did not conflict with his own interests — that is to say, with the interests of Spain as he saw them. Quixada's action in concealing the parentage of Don John from his wife was just the sort of loyal and unwise thing that might have been expected from a chivalrous knight, using the word "chivalrous" as it is commonly understood to-day; a dangerous thing, for many a woman would not have had sufficient faith in her husband to believe him when he suddenly produced an unexplained and charming little boy soon after he was married. Maddalena de Ulloa acted like an angel; Don Quixada acted like—Don Quixote! Now we see why I asked you particularly to note the name when we first came across it in the essay on Charles V. Whence did Cervantes get the idea for Don Quixote if not from the foster-father of Don John?

Two years later he got the real chance of his life. The Turks, having recovered from the shock inflicted on them by Charles V, captured Cyprus and seemed about to conquer all the little republics of the Adriatic. The Pope, Pius V, organized the "Holy League" between Spain and Venice, between the most fiercely monarchical of countries and the most republican of cities; and Don John was appointed Admiral-in-chief of the combined fleets of the "Last Crusade," as the enterprise is called from its mingled gallantry and apparent unity and idealism. For the last time men stood spellbound as Christendom attacked Mohammed.

> Strong gongs groaning as the guns boom far,
>
> And Don John of Austria is going to the war,

sings Chesterton in *Lepanto*, one of the most stirring battle-poems since the *Iliad*.

> Sudden and still—hurrah!
>
> Bolt from Iberia!
>
> Don John of Austria
>
> Is gone by Alcalar.

It is difficult for us nowadays to realize the terror of the Turks that possessed Europe in the sixteenth century; mothers quieted their children by the dreadful name, and escaped sailors recounted indescribable horrors in every little seaport from Albania to Scotland. Many thousands of Christian slaves laboured at the oars of the war-galleys, not, as is generally thought, as hostages that these galleys might not be sunk. They were the private property of the captains, who treated their own property better than they treated the property of the Grand Turk. Thus, it was not the worst fate for a Christian galley-slave to serve in the galley of his owner. He would not be exposed to reckless sinking at any rate; if the galley sank, it would be because the owner could not help it. Nor would he be likely to be impaled upon a red-hot poker or thrown upon butchers' hooks, as might happen to the slave of the Sultan. So it would seem that some unnecessary pity has been spilt upon the slaves of the galleys. Their lot might have been worse, to put things in their most favourable light.

King Philip's in his closet with the Fleece about his neck,

(Don John of Austria is armed upon the deck.)

Christian captives sick and sunless, all a labouring race repines

Like a race in sunken cities, like a nation in the mines.

(*"But Don John of Austria has burst the battle line!"*)

Don John pounding from the slaughter-painted poop,

Purpling all the ocean like a bloody pirate's sloop.

Vivat Hispania!

Domino gloria!

Don John of Austria

Has set his people free!

This "last crusade" culminated in the great battle of Lepanto, in 1571, where the Turks lost about 35,000 men and their whole battle fleet except forty galleys which crawled home disabled. There was a good deal of discussion about the action of an Italian galley under Doria, but Cervantes, in *Don Quixote*, seems to have been quite satisfied with it. No such wonderful battle was fought at sea until the Nile itself, which is the most perfect of all sea-fights.

The sensation throughout Europe was indescribable. Everything helped to make the victory romantic—the gallant young bastard admiral compared with the unattractive king under whom he served, the sudden relief from terrible danger, and the victory of Christ over Mahound, so dramatic and complete, all combined to stir the pulses of Christendom as they had never been stirred before—even in the earlier Crusades when the very tomb of Christ was the point under dispute. Men said that Mahound, when he heard the guns of Don John, wept upon the knees of his houris in his Paradise; black Azrael, the angel of death, had turned traitor upon his worshippers.

This glorious victory was won largely by the extraordinary daring and inspiring personality of the Emperor's bastard, who now, at the summit of human glory, saw himself condemned to retire into the position of a subject. The rest of the life of the "man who would be king" is the record of thwarted ambition and disappointed hopes. Spain and Venice quarrelled, and Lepanto was not followed up; Philip lost the chance of retrieving 1453 and of changing the history of Europe in Spain's favour ever since. Christian set once more to killing Christian in the old melancholy way; Venice made peace with the Sultan, and Don John set about carving out a kingdom for himself. In dreams he saw himself monarch of Albania, or of the Morea;

and in body he actually recaptured Tunis, once so gloriously held by his father. But Philip would not support him and he had to retire. Cervantes, in *Don Quixote*, evidently thinks Philip quite right. Tunis was a "sponge for extravagance, and a moth for expense; and as for holding it as a monument to Charles V, why, what monument was necessary to glory so eternal?" Don John returned home without a kingdom to his brother, who no doubt let him see that he was becoming rather a nuisance with his expensive dreams. In 1576 he was placated by an appointment as Governor-General to the Netherlands, where he quickly found himself confronted by a much greater, though less romantic, man than himself. William of Orange was now the unquestioned leader of the revolt of the Dutch against the Roman Catholic power of Philip, and when Don John reached the Netherlands he found himself Governor with no subjects. After fruitless negotiations he retired, a very ill man, to Namur; he had become thin and pale, and lost his vivacity. His heart was not in his task. He was meditating the extraordinary "empresa de Inglaterra" — the "enterprise of England" — which now seems to us so fantastic. The Spanish army was to evacuate the Netherlands and to be rapidly ferried across to Yorkshire; by a lightning stroke it was to release Mary Queen of Scots, that romantic Queen, and marry her to Don John, the romantic victor of Lepanto; Elizabeth was to be slain, and the Pope was to bless the union of romance with romance. But Elizabeth would have taken a deal of slaying. One cannot help surmising that Don John may have dreamed this fantasy because he had been educated by Quixada; it was a dream that might have passed through the addled brain of Don Quixote himself. The victor of Lepanto should better have understood the mighty power of the sea; the galleys which had done so well in the Mediterranean would have been worse than useless in the North, where the storms are a worse enemy than the Turks.

But Philip, either through timidity, or jealousy, or wisdom, would have none of it; after long delay he sent an important force to the Netherlands under the command of Don John's cousin, Alexander Farnese, Prince of Parma, the greatest general Spain ever produced. Don John abandoned his dreams to fall with this army upon the Protestants at Gemblours, where he, or Farnese — opinions differ — won a really great victory, the last that was to honour his name.

A curious incident in this campaign was that the Spaniards were attacked by a small Scottish force at a place called Rejnements. The Scotsmen began, *more Scotorum*, by singing a psalm. Having thus prepared the way spiritually, they prepared it physically by casting off their clothes, and to the horror of the modest Spaniards attacked naked with considerable success. Many of us, no doubt, remember how the Highlanders in the late war were said to have stained their bodies with coffee or Condy's fluid and, under cover of a Birnam's wood composed of branches of trees, emulated the bold Malcolm and Macduff by creeping upon the Germans attired mainly in their boots and identity disks; a sparse costume in which to appear before nursing sisters should they be wounded. I had the honour of operating upon one hefty gentleman who reached the C.C.S. in this attire, sheltered from the bitter cold by blankets supplied by considerate Australians in the field ambulance. We from a southern land considered the habit more suitable for the hardy Scot than for ourselves; though we remembered that an Australian surgeon at Gallipoli, finding that his dressings had run short, tore his raiment into strips and, when the need came, charged the Turks berserk attired in the costume of Adam before the Fall. But we did not remember that gallant Scotsmen had done something similar in 1578. No doubt the sight of a large man, dressed in cannibal costume and dancing horribly on the parapet while he poured forth a string of uncouth Doric imprecations, led to the tale that the British Army was employing African natives to devour the astonished Bosche.

Don John could not follow up the victory of Gemblours. He had neither money nor sufficient men; the few short months remaining to him were spent in imploring aid from his brother. Philip did nothing; possibly he was jealous of Don John; possibly he was fully occupied over the miserable affair of Antonio Perez and the Princess of Eboli. One would like to think that he had lucid intervals in which he recognized the insensate folly of the whole business; but like his father he was spurred on by his conscience. In addition to the other troubles of Don John his army began to waste away with pestilence, no doubt, it being now autumn, with typhoid, that curse of armies before the recent discovery of T.A.B. inoculation. Don John fell sick, in September, 1578, of a fever, but, his doctors considering the illness trifling, continued to work. One Italian, indeed, said that he would die, whereas another sick man, believed to be *in articulo mortis*, would recover. The guess proved right, and when Don John died the Italian surgeon's fortune was made. Thus easily are some reputations gained in our profession; it is easier to make a reputation than to keep it.

For nearly three weeks Don John struggled to work, encouraged by his physicians; there came a day, towards the end of September, when he, being already much wasted by his illness, was seized by a most violent pain and immediately had to go to bed. He became delirious, and babbled of battle-fields and trumpet-calls; he gave orders to imaginary lines of battle; he became unconscious. After two days of muttering delirium he awakened, and, as he was thought to be *in extremis*, took extreme unction. Next day the dying flicker continued, and he heard the priest say mass; though his sight had failed and he could not see, he had himself raised in the bed, feebly turned his head towards the elevation of the Host and adored the body of Christ with his last glimmer of consciousness. He then fell back unconscious, and sank into a state of coma, from which he never rallied. In all, he had been ill about twenty-four days.

These events could be easily explained on the supposition that this young man's brave life was terminated by that curse of young soldiers—ruptured typhoid ulcer in ambulatory typhoid fever. His army was dwindling with pestilence; he himself walked about feeling feverish and "seedy" and losing weight rapidly for a fortnight; he was just at the typhoid age, in the typhoid time of the year, and in typhoid conditions; his ulcer burst, causing peritonitis; the tremendous shock of the rupture, together with the toxæmia, drove him delirious and then unconscious; being a very strong young man he woke up again as the first shock passed away; as the shock passed into definite peritonitis unconsciousness returned, and he was fortunate in being able to hear his last mass before he died. I see no flaw in this reasoning.

The rest of the story is rather quaint. By next spring Philip had given orders for the embalmed body to be brought to Spain, and it was considered rather mean of him that the body of his brother was to be brought on mule-back. But Philip was at his wits' end for money to prosecute the war, and no doubt he himself looked upon his "meanness" as a wise economy. The body was exhumed, cut into three pieces—apparently by disjointing it at the hips—and stuffed into three leather bags which were slung on mule-back in a pack-saddle. When it came within a few miles of the Escorial it was put together again, laid upon a bier, and given a noble funeral in a death-chamber next to that which had been reserved for the great Emperor his father. There I believe it still lies, the winds of the Escorial laughing at its dreams of chivalrous glory.

Philip, suspicious of everybody and everything, had given orders that, should Don John die, his confessor was to keep an accurate record of the circumstances; and it is from the report of this priest that the above account has been drawn by Stirling-Maxwell, so we can look upon it as authoritative. Philip was accused of poisoning him, and for a moment this supposition was borne out by the extreme redness of the intestines; but this is much more easily explained by the peritonitis. Again, Philip's enemies have said that Don John died of a broken heart, because the priest reported that one side of his heart was dry and empty; but this too is quite natural if we suppose that the last act of Don John's life was for his heart to pump its blood into its arteries, as so often happens in death. Young men do not die of broken hearts; "Men have died and worms have eaten them—but not for love!" as Rosalind says in her sweet cynicism. In elderly men with high blood-pressures it is quite possible that grief and worry may actually cause the heart to burst, and to that extent novelists are right in speaking of a "broken heart." Otherwise the disease, or casualty, is unknown to medicine. No amount of worry, or absence of worry, would have had any effect upon Don John's typhoid ulcer.

Besides the suspicion of poisoning, Don John was rumoured to have died of the "French disease," even the name of the lady being mentioned. While he was certainly no more moral than any other gay and handsome young prince of his time, there is not the slightest reason for supposing the rumour to have been anything but folly. Syphilis does not kill a man as Don John died, while ambulatory typhoid fever most assuredly does. Therefore the lady in question must remain without her glory so far as this book is concerned, though her name has survived, and not only in Spanish.

Don John was a handsome young man, graceful and strong. There are many contemporary portraits of him, perhaps the best being a magnificent statue at Messina, which he saved from the Turks at Lepanto. He had frank blue eyes and yellow curls, and a very great charm of manner; but he was liable to attacks of violent pride which estranged his friends. He was the darling of the ladies, and was esteemed the flower of chivalry in his day; but William of Orange warned his Netherlanders not to be deceived by his appearance; in his view Philip had sent a monster of cruelty no less savage than himself. But William was prejudiced, and Don John is still one of the great romantic figures of history. It is difficult to speculate reasonably on what might have happened if he had not died. It has been thought that he might have led the Armada, in which case that most badly-managed expedition would at least have been well led, and no doubt England would have had a more determined struggle; but it seems to me more likely that Don John and Philip would have quarrelled, and that Fortune would have been even less kind to Spain than she was. Those who love Spain must be on the whole rather glad that Don John died before he had been able to cause more trouble than he did. It is difficult to agree entirely with those who would put the blame entirely on Philip for the troubles between him and Don John, or would interpret every act of Philip to his detriment. The whole story might be equally interpreted as the effort of a most conscientious and narrow-minded man endeavouring to follow out what he thought to be his father's wishes and at the same time to keep a wild young brother from kicking over the traces. Compare Butler's, *The Way of All Flesh*.

But the real interest to us of Don John is in his relations with Cervantes.

Cervantes on his galley puts his sword into its sheath

(*Don John of Austria rides homewards with a wreath*),

And he sees across a weary land a winding road in Spain

Up which a lean and foolish knight rides slowly up in vain.

And it will be a sad world indeed when Don Quixote at last reaches the top of that winding road and men cease to love him.

At Lepanto Miguel de Cervantes Saavedra (please pronounce the "a's" separately) was about twenty-five years of age, and was lying below deck sick of a fever. When he heard the roar of the guns of Don John he sprang from his bed and rushed on deck in spite of the orders of his captain; he was put in charge of a boat's crew of twelve men and went through the thick of the fighting. Every man in Don John's fleet was fired with his religious enthusiasm, and Cervantes' courage was only an index of the wild fervour that distinguished the Christians on that most bloody day. He was wounded in the left hand, "for the greater glory of the right," as he himself quaintly says, and never again could he move the fingers of the injured hand; no doubt the tendon sheaths had become septic, and he was lucky to have kept the hand at all. It has been sapiently remarked that the world would have had a great loss if it had been the right hand; but healthy people who lose the right hand can easily learn to write with the left. Cervantes remained in the fleet for some years until, on his way home, he was captured by Algerian pirates; put to the service of a Christian renegade—a man who had turned Mussulman to save his life or from still less worthy motive—Cervantes made several attempts to escape, but these were unsuccessful, and he remained in captivity for some years until his family had scraped up enough to ransom him. In *Don Quixote* there is a good deal about the renegadoes, and much of the well-known story of the "escaped Moor" is probably autobiographical; from these hints we gather that the renegadoes were not quite so bad as has been generally thought, or else that Cervantes was far too big-minded a man to believe unnecessary evil about anybody.

Back in Spain, he went into the army for two years, until, in 1582, he gave up soldiering and took to literature. He found the pen "a good stick but a bad crutch," and in 1585 returned to the public service as deputy-purveyor of the fleet. In 1594 he became collectors of revenues in Granada, and in 1597 he became short in his accounts and fell into jail. There he seems to have begun *Don Quixote*; he somehow obtained security for the repayment of the missing money, was released penniless into a suspicious world, and published the first part of *Don Quixote* in 1605. It was enormously well received, and from that day to this has remained one of the most successful of all books. Ten years later he found that dishonest publishers were issuing spurious second parts, so he sat himself down to write a genuine sequel. This differs from most sequels in that it is better than the original; it is wiser, mellower, less ironical; Don Quixote and Sancho Panza are still more lovable than they were before, and one imagines that Cervantes must have spent the whole ten years in collecting—or inventing—the wonderful proverbs so wisely uttered by the squire.

Though Cervantes wrote many plays he is now remembered mainly by his one very great romance, which is read lovingly in every language of every part of the world, so that the epithet "Quixotic" is applied everywhere to whatsoever is both gallant and foolish; an epithet which reflects the mixture of affection and pity in which the old Don is universally held, and is more often considered to be a compliment than the reverse. Curiously enough, women seldom seem to like Don Quixote; only the other day a brilliant young woman graduate told me that she thought he was a "silly old fool!" That was all she could see in him; but he is universally now thought to represent the pathos of the man who is born out of his time. As has been so well said, "This book is not meant for laughter—it is meant for tears." I can do no more than advise everybody to get a thin-paper copy and let it live in the pocket for some months, reading it at odd moments; it is the wisest and wittiest book ever published. "Blessed be the man who invented sleep," is a typical piece of Panzan philosophy with which most wise men will agree.

But when we have done sentimentalizing over the hidden meaning that undoubtedly underlies Don Quixote, we must not forget that it is extraordinarily funny even to a modern mind. The law that the humour of one generation is merely grotesque to the next does not seem to apply to *Don Quixote*; and I dare swear that the picture of the mad old Don, brought home from the inn of Maritornes, looking so stately in a cage upon a bullock-wagon, guarded by troopers of the Holy Brotherhood, and escorted by the priest and the barber, with the distracted Sancho Panza buzzing about wondering what has become of his promised Governorship, is absolutely the funniest thing in all literature; all the funnier because the springs of our laughter flow from the fount of our tears.

Now I cannot help thinking that when Cervantes began to write *Don Quixote* in prison, feeling bitter and sore against a world which had imprisoned him, and stiffened his hand for him, and condemned him to poverty and imprisonment, he must have had in his mind the story of the young bastard of Imperial Majesty who had risen to such heights of glory over Lepanto. It is not contended that Don Quixote was consciously intended to be a characterizature of Don Quixada or Don John, though his real name was Alonzo Quixana or Quixada, Don Quixote being a *nom de guerre* born of his frenzy; but I find it hard to believe that Cervantes had not heard of the foolish loyalty of Quixada in the matter of Jeronimo, or of the romantic dreams of Don John. It would seem that in these two incidents we find the true seeds of *Don Quixote*. It is not true that "Cervantes laughed Spain's chivalry away." Chivalry, meaning the social order of the true crusades, had long been dead even in Spain, the most conservative of nations. What really laughed Spain's chivalry away was the gay and joyous laugh of Don John himself, who would have plunged her into a great war for a dream. The man who seriously thought of dashing across the North Sea to marry Mary Queen of Scots would have been quite capable of tilting at windmills. In his inmost heart Cervantes must have seen his folly.

The death of Don Quixote is probably the most generally famous in literature, vying with that of Colonel Newcome, though more impressive because it is less sentimental. Cervantes had begun by rather jeering at his old Don, and subjecting him to uncalled-for cudgellings and humiliations; he then fell in love with the brave old lunatic, as everybody else has fallen in love with him ever since, and by the time that he came to die had drawn him as a really noble and beautiful character, who shows all the pathos of the idealist who is born out of his time. The death of Don Quixote is, except the death of one other Idealist, the most affecting death in all literature; the pathos is secured by means similarly restrained. The Bachelor Samson Carrasco, in his determination to cure Don Quixote of his knight-errant folly, had dressed himself up as "The Knight of the White Moon," and vowed that there was another lady more fair than Dulcinea del Toboso. At that blasphemy Don Quixote naturally flew to arms and challenged the insolent knight. By that time Rosinante was but old bones, so the Bachelor, being well-mounted on a young charger, overthrew the old horse and his brave old rider, and Don Quixote came to grass with a terrible fall. Then the Bachelor made Don Quixote vow that he would cease from his knight-errantry for a whole year, by which time it was hoped that he would be cured. They lifted his visor and found the old man "pale and sweating"; evidently Cervantes had seen some old man suffering from shock, and described what he saw in three words. From this humiliation Don Quixote never really recovered. He reached home and formed the mad idea of turning shepherd with Sancho and the Bachelor, and living out his penance in the fields. But Death saw otherwise, and the old man answered his call before he could do as he wished. He was seized with a violent fever that confined him to his room for six days; finally he slept calmly for some hours, and again awakened, only to fall into one attack of syncope after another until he died; the sanguine assurance of Sancho Panza that Dulcinea had been successfully disenchanted could not save him. Like most idealists he died a sad and disappointed man, certain of one thing only—that he was out of touch with the majority of mankind.

Cervantes was far too great an artist to kill his old hero by some such folly as "brain fever"—which nonsense I guess to have been typhoid. I believe that in describing the death of Don Quixote he was thinking of some old man whom he had seen crawl home to die after a severe physical shock, disappointed and disillusioned in a world of practical youth in which there is no room for romantic old age—probably some kind old man whom he himself had loved. These old men usually die of hypostatic pneumonia, which has been called the "natural end of man," and is probably the real broken heart of popular medicine. The old man, after a severe shock, is affected by a weakened circulation; the lungs are attacked by a slow inflammation, and he dies, usually in a few days, in much the same way as died Don Quixote. Cervantes did not know that these old men die from inflammation of the lungs; no doubt he observed the way they die, and immortalized his memories in the death of Don Quixote. I have written this to point out Cervantes' great powers of observation. He would probably have made a good doctor in our day.

This theory of *Don Quixote*, that at its roots lie memories of Don John and Don Quixada, is in no way inconsistent with Cervantes' own statement that he wrote the book to ridicule the romances of Chivalry which were so vitiating the literary taste of seventeenth-century Spain; at the back of his mind probably lay his own memories of foolish and gallant things, quite worthy of affectionate ridicule such as he has lavished on his knight-errant.

Philip II and the Arterio-Sclerosis
of Statesmen

WHEN the Empress Isabel was pregnant with the child which was to be Philip II, she bethought her of the glory that was hers in bearing offspring to a man so famous as the Roman Emperor, and she made up her mind that she would comport herself as became a Roman Empress. When, therefore, her relations and midwives during the confinement implored her to cry out or she would die, the proud Empress answered, "Die I may; but call out I *will not!*" and thus Philip arrived into the world sombre son of a stoical mother and heroic father. Doubtless she thought that she would show a courage equal to his father's, hoping that the son would then prove not unworthy. Though she was very beautiful, as Titian's famous portrait shows, she seems to have been a gloomy and austere woman, and Charles, being absent so long from her side at his wars, had to leave Philip's education mainly to her. His part consisted of many affectionate letters full of good and proud advice. Yet Philip grew up to be a merry little golden-haired boy enough, who rode about the streets of Toledo in a go-cart amidst the crowds that we are told pressed to see the Emperor's son. The calamity of his life was that Charles had bequeathed to him the kingdom of the Netherlands. Charles himself was essentially a Fleming, who got on exceedingly well with his brother Flemings, Reformation or no Reformation; they were quite prepared to admit that the great man might have some good reason for his religious persecution, peculiar though it no doubt seemed. But Philip was a foreigner; and a foreigner of the race of Torquemada who, so they heard, had so strengthened the Inquisition less than a century before that now it was really not safe to think aloud in matters of religion. So the Dutch rose in revolt under William of Orange, and the Dutch Republic came into being. Philip was only able to save the southern Netherlands from the wreck, which ultimately formed the kingdom of Belgium. Philip always thought that if he could only get England on his side the pacification of the Netherlands would be easy; so, at the earnest request of Charles, he married Mary Tudor, a woman twelve years older than himself, a marriage which turned out unhappily from every point of view, and has wrongly coloured our general opinion of Philip's character. The unfortunate attempt to conquer England by the Armada, a fleet badly equipped and absurdly led, has also led us to despise both him and his Spaniards, whence came the general English schoolboy idea that the Spanish were a nation of braggarts ruled by a murderous fool, whose only thirst was for Protestant gore. But this idea was very far from being true. Philip was no fool; he was an exceedingly learned, conscientious, hard-working, careful, and painstaking bureaucrat, who might have done very well indeed had he been left the kingdom of Spain alone; but had no power of attracting foreigners to his point of view. He always did his best according to his lights; and if his policy sometimes appears tortuous to us, that is simply because we forget that it was then thought perfectly right for kings to do tortuous things for the sake of their people, just as to-day party leaders sometimes do extraordinarily wicked things for the sake of what they consider the principles of their party. Unfortunately for Philip he often failed in his efforts; and the man who fails is always in the wrong.

He was constantly at war, sometimes unsuccessfully, often victoriously. Unlike Charles he did not lead his armies in person, but sat at home and prayed, read the crystal, and organized. After the great battle of St. Quentin, in which he defeated the French, he vowed to erect a mighty church to the glory of St. Lawrence which should excel every other building in the world; and for thirty years the whole available wealth of Spain and the Indies was poured out on the erection of the Escorial, which the Spaniards look upon as the eighth wonder of the world, and who is to say that they are wrong? Situated about twenty miles from Madrid, in a bleak and desolate mountain range, it reflects extraordinarily well the character of the man who made it. Under one almost incredible roof it combines a palace, a university, a monastery, a church, and a mausoleum. The weight of its keys alone is measured in scores of pounds; the number of its windows and its doors is counted in hundreds; it contains the greatest works of many very great artists, and the tombs of Charles V and his descendants. It stands in lonely grandeur swept by constant bitter winds, a fit monument for a lonely and morose king. Its architecture is Doric, and stern as its own granite.

The character of Philip II has been described repeatedly, in England mainly by his enemies, who have laid too much stress on his cruelty and bigotry. Though he was fiercely religious, yet he loved art and wrote poetry; though he would burn a heretic as blithely as any man, yet he was a kind husband to his four wives, whom he married one after the other for political reasons; though he was gloomy and austere, yet he loved music, and was moved almost to tears by the sound of the nightingale in the summer evenings of Spain. His people loved him and affectionately called him "Philip the prudent"; they forgave him his mistakes, for they knew that he worked always for the ancient religion which they loved, and for the glory of Spain.

Unlike Charles his father, he was austere in his mode of life, and always had a doctor at his side at meals lest he should forget his gout. He was a martyr to that most distressing complaint, no doubt inherited from his father. He lived abstemiously, but took too little exercise; it would have been better for his health—and probably for the world—had he followed his armies on horseback like Charles, even if he had recognized that he was no great general.

His death, at the age of seventy-two, was proud and sombre, as befitted the son of the Empress Isabel, who had scorned to cry when he was born. We can understand a good deal about Philip if we consider him as spiritually the son of that proud sombre woman rather than of his glorious and energetic father. In June, 1598, he was attacked by an unusually severe attack of gout which so crippled him that he could hardly move. He was carried from Madrid to the Escorial in a litter, and was put to bed in a little room opening off the church so that he could hear the friars at their orisons. Soon he began to suffer from "malignant tumours" all over his legs, which ulcerated, and became intensely painful, so that he could not bear even a wet cloth to be laid upon them or to have the ulcers dressed. So he lay for fifty-three days suffering frightful tortures, but never uttering a word of complaint, even as his mother had borne him in silence for the sake of the great man who had begotten him. As the ulcers could not be dressed, they naturally became covered with vermin and smelled horribly. Stoical in his agony, he called his son before him, apologizing for doing so, but it was necessary. "I want," he said, "to show you how even the greatest monarchies must end. The crown is slipping from my head, and will soon rest upon yours. In a few days I shall be nothing but a corpse swathed in its winding-sheet, girdled with a rope." He showed no sign of emotionalism, but retained his self-control to the last; after he had said farewell to his son he considered that he had left the world, and devoted the last few days of his life to the offices of the church. The monks in the church wanted to cease the continual dirges and services, but he insisted that they should go on, saying: "The nearer I get to the fountain, the more thirsty I become!"

These seem to have been his last words; he appears to have retained consciousness as long as may be.

Let us reason together and try if we can make head or tail of this extraordinary illness. The first certain fact about Philip II is that he long suffered from gout, apparently the real old-fashioned gout in the feet. In the well-known picture of him receiving a deputation of Netherlanders, as he sits in his tall hat beneath a crucifix, it is perfectly evident that he is suffering tortures from gout and wearing a large loosely fitting slipper. These unfortunate gentlemen seem to have selected a most unpropitious moment to ask favours, for there is no ailment that so warps the temper as gout. When a man suffers from gout over a period of years it is only a matter of time till his arteries and kidneys go wrong and he gets arterio-sclerosis. We may take it, therefore, as certain that at the age of seventy-two Philip had sclerosed arteries and probably chronic Bright's disease like his father before him. Gout, Bright's disease, and high blood-pressure, are all strongly hereditary, as every insurance doctor knows; that is to say, the son of a father who has died of one of these three is more likely than not to die ultimately of some cognate disease of arteries or kidneys or heart, all grouped together under the name of cardio-vascular-renal disease.

But what about the "malignant tumours"? "Malignant tumour" to-day means cancer of one sort or another, and assuredly it was not cancer that killed Philip. Probably the word "tumour" simply meant "swelling." Now, what could these painful swellings have been which ulcerated and smelt so horribly? Why not gangrene? Ordinary senile gangrene, such as occurs in arterio-sclerosis, neither causes swellings, nor is it painful, nor does it smell nor become verminous; but diabetic gangrene does all these things. Diabetes in elderly people may go on for many years undiscovered unless the urine be chemically examined, and may only cause symptoms when the arterio-sclerosis which generally complicates it gives results, such as sudden death from heart-failure, or diabetic gangrene. Thus a very famous Australian statesman, who had been known to have sugar in his urine for many years, was one morning found dead in his bath, evidently due to the high blood-pressure consequent on diabetic arterio-sclerosis.

Diabetic gangrene often begins in some small area of injured skin, such as might readily occur in a foot tortured with gout; it ulcerates, is exceedingly painful, and possessed of a stench quite peculiar to its horrid self. It does not confine itself to one foot, or to one area of a leg, but suddenly appears in an apparently healthy portion, having surreptitiously worked its way along beneath the skin; its first sign is often a painful swelling which ulcerates. The patient dies either from toxæmia due to the gangrene, or from diabetic coma; and fifty-three days is not an unlikely period for the torture to continue. On the whole it would seem that diabetic gangrene appearing in a man who has arterio-sclerosis is a probable explanation of Philip's death. The really interesting part of this historical diagnosis is the way in which it explains his treatment of the Netherlands. What justice could they have received from a man tortured and rendered petulant with gout and gloomy with diabetes?

Charles V had taken no care of himself, but had gone roaring and fighting and guzzling and drinking all over Europe; Philip had led a very quiet, studious, and abstemious life, and therefore he lived nearly twenty years longer than his father. Possibly when he came to suffer the torments of his death he may have thought the years not worth his self-denial: possibly he may have regretted that he did not have a good time when he was young, but this is not likely, for he was a very conscientious man.

When Philip lay dying he held in his hand the common little crucifix that his mother and father had adored when they too had died; his friends buried it upon his breast when they came to inter him in the Escorial, where it still lies with him in a coffin made of the timbers of the *Cinco Chagas*, not the least glorious of his fighting galleys.

Arterio-sclerosis, high blood-pressure, hyperpiesis, and chronic Bright's disease—all more or less names for the same thing, or at any rate for cognate disorders—form one of the great tragedies of the world. They attack the very men whom we can least spare; they are essentially the diseases of statesmen. Although these diseases have been attributed to many causes—that is to say, we do not really know their true cause—it is certain that worry has a great deal to do with them. If a man be content to live the life of a cabbage, eat little, and drink no alcohol, it is probable that he will not suffer from high blood-pressure; but if he is determined to work hard, live well, and yet struggle furiously, then his arteries and kidneys inevitably go wrong and he is not likely to stand the strain for many years. Unless a politician has an iron nerve and preternaturally calm nature, or unless he is fortunate enough to be carried off by pneumonia, then he is almost certain to die of high blood-pressure if he persists in his politics. I could name a dozen able politicians who have fallen victims to their political anxieties. The latest, so far as I know, was Mr. John Storey, Premier of New South Wales, who died of high blood-pressure in 1921; before him I remember several able men whom the furious politics of that State claimed as victims. In England Lord Beaconsfield seems to have died of high blood-pressure, and so did Mr. Joseph Chamberlain. Mr. Gladstone was less fortunate, in that he died of cancer. He must have possessed a calm mind to go through his furious strugglings without his kidneys or blood-vessels giving way; that, and his singularly temperate and happy home-life, preserved him from the usual fate of statesmen.

Charles V differed from Mr. Gladstone because he habitually ate far too much, and could never properly relax his mental tension. His arterio-sclerosis had many results on history. It was probably responsible for his extreme fits of depression, in one of which it pleased Fate that he should meet Barbara Blomberg. If he had not been extraordinarily depressed and unhappy, owing to his arterio-sclerosis, he would probably not have troubled about her, and there would have been no Don John of Austria. If he had not had arterio-sclerosis he would probably not have abdicated in

1556, when he should have had many years of wise and useful activities before him. If his judgment had not been warped by his illness he would probably never have appointed Philip II to be his successor as King of the Netherlands; he would have seen that the Dutch were not the sort of people to be ruled by an alien. And if there had been no Don John it is possible that there would have been no Don Quixote. Once again, if Philip had not been eternally preoccupied with his senseless struggle against the Dutch, it is probable that he would have undertaken his real duty—to protect Europe from the Turk. When one considers how the lives of Charles and his sons might have been altered had his arteries been carrying a lower blood-tension, it rather tends to alter the philosophy of history to a medical man.

Again, when we consider that the destinies of nations are commonly held in the hands of elderly gentlemen whose blood-pressures tend to be too high owing to their fierce political activities, it is not too much to say that arterio-sclerosis is one of the greatest tragedies that afflict the human race. Every politician should have his blood-pressure tested and his urine examined about once a quarter, and if it should show signs of rising he should undoubtedly take a long rest until it falls again; it is not fair that the lives of millions should depend upon the judgment of a man whose mind is warped by arterio-sclerosis.

Mr. and Mrs. Pepys

SAMUEL PEPYS, Father of the Royal Navy, and the one man—if indeed there were any one man—who made possible the careers of Blake and Nelson, died in 1703 in the odour of the greatest respectability. Official London followed him to his honoured grave, and he left behind him the memory of a great and good servant of the King in "perriwig" (alas, to become too famous), stockings and silver buckles. But unhappily for his reputation, though greatly to the delight of a wicked world, he had, during ten momentous years, kept a diary. It was written in a kind of shorthand which he seems to have flattered himself would not be interpreted; but by some extraordinary mischance he had left a key amongst his papers. Early in the nineteenth century part of the Diary was translated, and a part published. A staggered world asked for more, and during the next three generations further portions were made public, until by this time nearly the whole has been published, and it is unlikely that the small remaining portions will ever see the light.

Pepys seems to have set down every thought that came into his head as he wrote; things which the ordinary man hardly admits to himself— even supposing that he ever thinks or does them—this stately Secretary of the Navy calmly wrote in black and white with a garrulous effrontery that absolutely disarms criticism. In its extraordinary self-revelation the Diary is unique; it is literally true that there is nothing else like it in any other language, and it is almost impossible that anything like it will ever be written again; the man, the moment, and the occasion can never recur. I take it that every man who presumes to call himself educated has at least a nodding acquaintance with this immortal work; but a glance at some of its medical features may be interesting. The difficulties at this end of the world are considerable, because the Editor has veiled some of the more interesting medical passages in the decent obscurity of asterisks, and one has to guess at some anatomical terms which, if too Saxon to be printable in modern English, might very well have been given in technical Latin. Let us begin with a brief study of the delightful woman who had the good fortune—or otherwise—to be Pepys's wife. Daughter of a French immigrant and an Irish girl, Elizabeth Pepys was married at fourteen, and her life ended, after fifteen somewhat hectic years, in 1669, when she was only twenty-nine years of age. Pepys repeatedly tells us that she was pretty—and no one was ever a better judge than he—and "very good company when she is well." Her portrait shows her with a bright, clever little face, her upper lip perhaps a trifle longer than the ideal, bosom well developed, and a coquettish curl allowed to hang over her forehead after the fashion of the Court of Charles II. She spoke and read French and English; she took the keenest interest in life, and set to work to learn from her husband arithmetic, "musique," the flageolet, use of the globes, and various accomplishments which modern girls learn at school. Mrs. Pepys imbibing all this erudition from her husband, while her pretty little dog lies snoring on the mat, forms a truly delightful picture, and no doubt our imagination of it is no more delightful than the reality was three hundred years ago. I suppose it was the same dog as he whose puppyish indiscretions had led to many a fierce quarrel between husband and wife; Pepys always carefully recorded these indiscretions, both of the dog and, alas, of himself. It is clear that the sanitary conveniences in Pepys's house could not have been up to his requirements.

Husband and wife went everywhere together, and seem really to have loved each other; the impression that I gather from Pepys's exceedingly candid description of her is that she was a loyal and comradely wife, with a spirit of her own, and a good deal to put up with; for though Pepys was continually—and causelessly—jealous of her, yet he did not hold that he was in any way bound to be faithful to her on his own side. So they pass through life, Pepys philandering with every attractive woman who came his way, and Mrs. Pepys dressing herself prettily, learning her little accomplishments, squabbling with her maids, and looking after her house and his meals, till one day she engaged a servant, Deb Willet by name, who brought a touch of tragedy into the home. In November, 1668, Deb was combing Pepys's hair— no doubt in preparation for the immortal "perriwig"—when Mrs. Pepys came in and caught him "embracing her," thus occasioning "the greatest sorrow to me that ever I knew in this world," as he puts it.

Mrs. Pepys was "struck mute," and was silently furious. Outraged Juno towered over the unhappy Pepys, and so to bed without a word, nor slept all night; but about two in the morning Juno became very woman; woke him up and told him she had "turned Roman Catholique," this being, in the state of politics at that time, probably the thing which she thought would hurt him more than anything else she could say. For the next few days Pepys is sore troubled, and his usual genial babble becomes almost incoherent. The wrong dating and the expressions of "phrenzy" show the mental agony that he passed through, and there can be no doubt that the joy of life passed out of him, probably never more fully to return. The rest of the Diary is written in a style graver than at first—some of it is almost passionate. He describes with much mental agitation how he woke up in the middle of one night, and found his wife heating a pair of tongs red-hot and preparing to pinch his nose; gone for ever were the glad days when he could pull her nose, and the "poor wretch" thought none the worse of the lordly fellow. Twice had he done so, and, as he says, "to offend." One would like to have Mrs. Pepys's account of this nose-pulling, and what she really thought of it. Some people have found the struggle of Pepys to cure himself of his infatuation for Deb humorous; to any ordinarily sympathetic soul who reads how he prayed on his knees in his own room that God would give him strength never again to be unfaithful, and how he appealed again and again to his wife to forgive him, and how he, to the best of his ability, avoided the girl, the whole business becomes rather too painful to be funny, even though the unhappy man has the art of making himself ridiculous in nearly every sentence. Finally, in a fury of jealousy, she forced him to write a most insulting letter to Miss Willet, a letter that no woman could ever possibly forgive, and Pepys's life appears to have settled down again. His sight failing him[9] — it is thought that he suffered from hypermetropia combined with early presbyopia — he abandoned the Diary just at the time when one would have dearly liked to hear more; and we never hear the end either of Deb or of their married happiness. Reading between the lines, one gathers that probably Deb was more sinned against than sinning, and that Mrs. Pepys had more real reason to be angry about many women of whom she had never heard than about the young woman whose flirtation was the actual *casus belli*. It is an unjust world. The two went abroad for a six-months' tour in France and Holland, and immediately after they returned Mrs. Pepys fell ill of a fever; for a time she appears to have fought it well, but she took a bad turn and died. Considering her youth, the season of the year, and that they had just returned from the Continent, the disease was possibly typhoid. Pepys erected an affectionate memorial to her, and was later on buried by her side. He took the last sacrament with her as she lay dying, so we may reasonably suppose that she died having forgiven him, and it is not unfair to imagine that the trip abroad was a second honeymoon. They were two grown-up children, playing with life as with a new toy.

Mrs. Pepys was liable to attacks of boils in asterisks; and a Dr. Williams acquired considerable merit by supplying her with plasters and ointments. On November 16, 1663, "Mr. Hollyard came, and he and I about our great work to look upon my wife's malady, which he did, and it seems her great conflux of humours heretofore that did use to swell there did in breaking leave a hollow which has since gone in further and further till it is now three inches deep, but as God will have it did not run into the body-ward, but keeps to the outside of the skin, and so he will be forced to cut open all along, and which my heart will not serve me to see done, and yet she will not have no one else to see it done, no, not even her mayde, and so I must do it poor wretch for her." Pepys is in a panic at the thought of assisting at the opening of this subcutaneous abscess; one can feel the courage oozing out at the palms of his hands as one reads his agitated words. To his joy, next morning Mr. Hollyard, on second thoughts, "believes a fomentation will do as well, and what her mayde will be able to do as well without knowing what it is for, but only that it is for the piles." Evidently the "mayde's" opinion was of some little moment in Mrs. Pepys's censorious world. Mr. Pepys would have been much troubled to see his wife cut before his face: "he could not have borne to have seen it." Mr. Hollyard received £3 "for his work upon my wife, but whether it is cured or not I cannot say, but he says it will never come to anything, but it may ooze now and again." Mr. Hollyard was evidently easily satisfied. Of course, there must have been a sinus running in somewhere, but it is impossible to guess at its origin. Possibly some pelvic sepsis; possibly an ischio-rectal abscess. A long time before he had noted that his wife was suffering from a "soare belly," which may possibly have been the beginning of the trouble, but there is no mention of any long and serious illness such as usually accompanies para-metric sepsis. On the whole, I fancy ischio-rectal abscess to be the most likely explanation. Later on she suffers from abscesses in the cheek, which "by God's mercy burst into the mouth, thus not spoiling her face"; and she had constant trouble with her teeth. It is thus quite probable that the origin of the whole illness may have been pyorrhœa, and no doubt this would go hard with her in the fever from which she died. Possibly this may have been septic pneumonia arising from septic foci in the mouth; but, after all, it is idle to speculate.

Mrs. Pepys never became pregnant during the period covered by the Diary, though there were one or two false alarms. There is no mention of any continuous or constant ill-health, such as we find in pyo-salpinx or severe tubal adhesions; and such being the case, her sterility may quite likely have been as much his fault as hers.

One cannot read the Diary without wishing that we could have heard a little more of her side of the questions that arose. What did she really think of her husband when he pulled her nose? Twice, too, no less! Stevenson calls her "a vulgar woman." Stevenson's opinion on every matter is worthy of the highest respect, as that of a sensitive, refined, and artistic soul; but I cannot help thinking that sometimes his early Calvinistic training tended to make him rather intolerant to human weakness. His judgment of François Villon always seems to me intolerant and unjust, and he showed no sign in his novels of ever having made any effort to comprehend the difficulties and troubles which surround women in their passage through the world. He understood men—there can be no doubt of that; but I doubt if he understood women even to the small extent which is achieved by the average man. Personally I find Mrs. Pepys far from "vulgar"; generally she is simply delightful. True, one cannot concur with her action over the letter to Deb. It was cruel and ungenerous. But she probably knew her husband well by that time, and judged fairly accurately the only thing that would be likely to bring him up with a round turn, and again we have not the privilege of knowing Deb except through Pepys's possibly too favourable eyes. Deb may have been all that Mrs. Pepys thought her, and she may have richly deserved what she got. After all, there is in every woman protecting her husband from the onslaughts of "vamps" not a little of the wild-cat. Even the gentlest of women will defend her husband—especially a husband who retains so much of the boy as Pepys—from the attempts of wicked women to steal him, poor innocent love, from her sacred hearth; will defend him with bare hands and claws, and totally regardless of the rules of combat; and it is this touch of cattishness in Mrs. Pepys which makes one's heart warm towards her. For all we know Deb Willet may have been a "vamp." Mrs. Pepys was certainly the "absolute female."

Mr. Pepys suffered from stone in the bladder before he began to keep a diary. He does not appear to have been physically a hero; had he been a general, no doubt he would have led his army bravely from the rear except in case of a retreat; but so great was the pain that he submitted his body to the knife on March 26, 1658. Anæsthetics in those days were rudimentary, relaxing rather than anæsthetizing the patient. There is some reason to believe that they were extensively used in the Middle Ages, and contemporaries of Shakespeare seem to have looked on their use as a matter of course; but for some reason they became less popular, and by the seventeenth century most people had to undergo their operations with little assistance beyond stout hearts and sluggish nervous systems.

Cutting for the stone was one of the earliest of surgical operations. In ancient days it was first done in India, and the glad news that stones could be successfully removed from the living body filtered through to the Greeks some centuries before Christ. Hippocrates knew all about it, and the operation is mentioned in that Hippocratic oath according to which some of us endeavour to regulate our lives. At first it was only done in children, because it was considered that adult men would not heal properly, and the only result in them would be a fistula. The child was held on the lap of some muscular assistant, with one or two not less muscular men holding its arms and legs. The surgeon put one or two fingers into the little anus and tried to push the stone down on to the perineum, helped in this manœuvre by hypogastric pressure from another assistant. He then cut transversely above the anus, strong in the faith that he might, if the gods willed, open into the neck of the bladder. Next he tried to push out the stone with his fingers still in the anus; it is not quite clear whether he would take his fingers out of the anus and put them into the wound or vice versa; this failing, he would seize the stone with forceps and drag it through the perineum. As time went on it was discovered that more than three or four assistants could be employed, using others to sit on the patient's chest, thus adding the *peine forte et dure* to the legitimate terrors of ancient surgery and surrounding him with a mass of men. Imbued with a spirit of unrest by the struggles of the patient the mass swayed this way and that, until it was discovered that by adding yet more valiants to the wings of the "scrum," who should answer heave with counter-heave, the resultant of the opposing forces would hold even the largest perineum steady enough for the surgeon to operate; and men came under the knife for stone. Next the patient was tied up with ropes, somewhat in the style we used in our boyhood's sport of cock-fighting. What a piece of work is the Rope! How perfect in all its works—from the Pyramids—built with the aid of the Rope and the Stick—to the execution of the latest murderer. One might write pages on the influence of the Rope on human progress; but for our purpose we may simply say that probably Mr. Pepys was kept quiet with many yards of hemp. Those who cut for the stone were specialists, doing nothing else; their arrival at a patient's house must have resembled an invasion, with their vast armamentarium and crowds of assistants. By Pepys's time Marianus Sanctus had lived—yes, so greatly was he venerated that they called him "Sanctus," the Holy Man; Saint Marianus if you will. He it was, in Italy in 1524, who invented the apparatus major, which made the operation a little less barbarous than that of the Greeks. This God-sent apparatus consisted mainly of a grooved staff to be shoved into the bladder and a series of forceps. You cut on to the staff as the first step of the operation; it was believed that if you cut in the middle line in the raphe the wound would never heal, owing to the callosity of the part; moreover, if you carried your incision too far back you would cause fatal hæmorrhage from the inferior hæmorrhoidal veins. Having, then, made your incision well to the right or left, you exposed the urethra, made a good big hole in that pipe, and inserted a fine able pair of tongs, with which you seized hold of the stone and crushed it if you could, pulling it out in bits; or if the stone were hard, and you had preternaturally long fingers, you might even get it out on a finger-tip. It was always considered the mark of a wise surgeon to carry a spare stone with him in his waistcoat pocket, so that the patient might at least have a product of the chase to see if the surgeon should find his normal efforts unrewarded. Diagnosis was little more advanced in those days than operative surgery; there are numbers of conditions which may have caused symptoms like those of a stone, and it was always well for the surgeon to be prepared.

This would be the operation that was performed on Mr. Pepys. The results in many cases were disastrous; some men lost control of their sphincter vesicæ; many were left with urinary fistulæ; in many the procreative power was permanently destroyed by interference with the seminal vesicles and ducts. Probably some of us would prefer to keep our calculi rather than let a mediæval stone-cutter perform upon us; we are a degenerate crew. It is not altogether displeasing to imagine the roars of the unhappy Pepys, trussed and helpless, a pallid little Mrs. Pepys quaking outside the door, perhaps not entirely sorry that her own grievances were being so adequately avenged, although the vengeance was vicarious; while the surgeon wrestled with a large uric acid calculus which could with difficulty be dragged through the wound. It is all very well for us to laugh at the forth-right methods of our ancestors; but, considering their difficulties—no anæsthesia, no antiseptics, want of sufficient surgical practice, and the fact that few could ever have had the hardness of heart necessary to stand the patient's bawlings, it is remarkable that they did so well and that the mortality of this appalling operation seems only to have been from 15 to 20 per cent. Moreover we may be pretty sure that no small stone would ever be operated upon; men postponed the operation until the discomfort became intolerable. It remained for the genius of Cheselden, when Pepys was dead and possibly in heaven some twenty years, to devise the operation of lateral lithotomy, one of the greatest advances ever made in surgery. This operation survived practically unchanged till recent times.

Pepys's heroism was not in vain, and was rewarded by a long life free from serious illness till the end. March 26 became to him a holy day, and was kept up with pomp for many years. The people of the house wherein he had suffered and been strong were invited to a solemn feast on that blessed day, and as the baked meats went round and the good wine glowed in the decanters, Mr. Pepys stood at his cheer and once again recounted the tale of his agony and his courage. Nowadays, when we are operated upon with little more anxiety than we should display over signing a lease, it is difficult to imagine a state of things such as must have been inevitable in the days before Simpson and Lister.

The stone re-formed, but not in the bladder. Once you have a uric acid calculus you can never be quite sure you have done with it until you are dead, and in the case of Mr. Pepys recurrence took place in the kidney. When he died, an old man, in 1703, they performed a post-mortem examination on his body, suspecting that his kidneys were at fault, and in the left kidney found a nest of no less than seven stones, which must have been silently growing in the calyces for unnumbered years. Nor does it seem to me impossible that his extraordinary incontinence—he never seems to have been able to resist any feminine allurement, however coarse—may really have been due to the continued irritation of the old scar in his perineum. There is often a physical condition as the basis for this type of character, and some trifling irritation may make all the difference between virtue and concupiscence. This reasoning is probably more likely to be true than much of the psychoanalysis which is at present so fashionable among young ladies. Possibly also the sterility of Mrs. Pepys may have been partly due to the effects of the operation upon her husband.

One unpleasant result to Mr. Pepys was the fact that whenever he crossed his legs carelessly he became afflicted with a mild epididymitis—he describes it much less politely himself, doubtless in wrath. His little failing in this respect must have been a source of innocent merriment to the many friends who were in the secret. He was also troubled with attacks of severe pain whenever the weather turned suddenly cold. At first he used to be in terror lest his old enemy had returned, but he learned to regard the attacks philosophically as part of the common heritage of mankind, for man is born to trouble as the sparks fly upward. Probably they were due to reflex irritation from the stones growing in the kidney. He does not seem to have passed any small stones per urethram, or he would assuredly have told us. He took great interest in his own emunctories—probably other people's, too, from certain dark sayings.

Considering the by no means holy living of Mr. Pepys, it is rather remarkable that he never seems to have suffered from venereal disease, and this leads me to suspect that possibly these ailments were not so common in the England of the Restoration as they are to-day. It seems impossible that any man could live in Sydney so promiscuously as Mr. Pepys without paying the penalty; and the experience of our army in London seems to show that things there must be much the same as here (Sydney). I often wonder whether Charles II and his courtiers were really representative of the great mass of people in England at that time; probably the prevalence of venereal disease in modern times is due to the enormous increase in city life; probably men and women have always been very much the same from generation to generation—inflammable as straw, given the opportunities which occur mainly in cities and crowded houses.

Ignoble as was Pepys, he yet showed real moral courage during the Plague. When that great enemy of cities attacked London he, very wisely, sent his family into the country at Woolwich, while he remained faithful to his duty and continued to work at the navy in Greenwich, Deptford, and London. I cannot find in the Diary any mention of any particular attraction that kept him in London during those awful five months; he would, no doubt, have mentioned her name if there had been such; yet candour compels me to observe that there was seldom any one attraction for Mr. Pepys, unless poor Deb Willet may have somehow mastered—temporarily—his wayward heart. But, as might have been expected, he was little more virtuous during his wife's absence than before; indeed, possibly the imminent danger of death may have led him to enjoy his life while yet he might, with his usual fits of agonized remorse, whose effects upon his conduct were brief. We owe far more to his organizing power and honesty—not a bigoted variety—than is generally remembered. His babble is not the best medium for vigorous description, and you will not get from Pepys any idea of the epidemic comparable with that which you will get from the journalist Defoe; yet through those months there lurks a feeling of horror which still impresses mankind. The momentary glimpse of a citizen who stumbles over the "corps" of a man dead of the plague, and running home tells his pregnant wife; she dies of fear forthwith; a man, his wife, and three children dying and being buried on one day; persons quick to-day and dead to-morrow—not in scores, but in hundreds; ten thousand dying in a week; the horrid atmosphere of fear and suspicion which overlay London; and Pepys himself setting his papers in order, so that men might think well of him should it please the Lord to take him suddenly: all give us a sense of doom all the more poignant because recently we went through a much milder version of the same experience ourselves. The papers talked glibly of the influenza as "The Plague." How different it was from the real bubonic plague is shown by the statistics. In five months of 1665 there died of the plague in the little London of that day no less than about 70,000 people, according to the bills of mortality; in truth, probably far more; that is to say, probably a fifth of the people perished. There is no doubt that the bubonic plague kept back the development of cities, and therefore of civilization, for centuries, and that the partial conquest of the rat has been one of the greatest achievements of the human race. What is happening in Lord Howe Island, where it is exceedingly doubtful whether rats or men shall survive in that beautiful speck of land, shows how slender is the hold which mankind has upon the earth; and wherever the rat is able to breed unchecked, man is liable to sink back into savagery. The rat, the tubercle bacillus, and the bacillus of typhoid are the three great enemies of civilization; we hold our position against them at the price of eternal vigilance, and probably the rat is not the least deadly of these enemies.

I need not go through the Diary in search of incidents; most of them, while intensely amusing, are rather of interest to the psychologist in the study of self-revelation than to the medical man. When Pepys's brother lay dying the doctor in charge hinted that possibly the trouble might have been of syphilitic origin; Pepys was virtuously wrathful, and the unhappy doctor had to apologize and was forthwith discharged. I cannot here narrate how they proved that the unhappy patient had never had syphilis in his life; you must read the Diary for that. Their method would not have satisfied either Wassermann or Bordet. Another time Pepys was doing something that he should not have been doing at an open window in a draught; the Lord punished him by striking him with Bell's palsy. Still again, at another time he got something that seems to have resembled pseudo-ileus, possibly reflex from his latent calculi. Everybody in the street was much distressed at his anguish; all the ladies sent in prescriptions for enemata; the one which relieved him consisted of small beer! Indeed, one marvels always at the extraordinary interest shown by Pepys's lady-friends in his most private ailments. London must have been a friendly little town in the seventeenth century, in the intervals of hanging people and chopping off heads.

But the great problem remains: Why did Pepys write down all these intimate details of his private life? Why did he confess to things which most men do not confess even to themselves? Why did he write it all down in cypher? Why, when he narrated something particularly disgraceful, did he write in a mongrel dialect of bad French, Italian, Spanish, and Latin? He could not have seriously believed that a person who was able to read the Diary would not be able to read the very simple foreign words with which it is interspersed. Most amazing of all: Why did he keep the manuscript for more than thirty years, a key with it? One thinks of the fabled ostrich who buries his head in the sand. The problem of Pepys still remains unsolved, in spite of the efforts of Stevenson in *Familiar Studies of Men and Books*. Stevenson was the last man in the world to understand Pepys, but more competent exegetists have tried and failed. One can only say that his failing sight—which Professor Osborne of Melbourne attributes to astigmatism—has deprived the world of a treasure that can never be sufficiently regretted. No man can be considered educated who has not read at least part of the Diary; in no other way is it possible to get so vivid a picture of the ordinary people of a past age; as we read they seem to live before us, and it comes as a shock to remember that poor Pall Pepys—his plain sister—and "my wife" and Mrs. Batelier—"my pretty valentine"—and Sir William Coventry and Mercer, and the hundreds more who pass so vividly before us, are all dead these centuries.

If this little paper shall send some to the reading of this most extraordinary book, I shall be more than satisfied. The only edition which is worth while is Wheatley's, in ten volumes, with portraits and a volume of *Pepysiana*. The smaller editions are apt to transmute Pepys into an ordinary humdrum and industrious civil servant.

Edward Gibbon

FOR many years it has been taught—I have taught it myself to generations of students—that Gibbon's hydrocele surpassed in greatness all other hydroceles, that it contained twelve pints of fluid, and that it was, in short, one of those monstrous things which exist mainly in romance; one of those chimeras which grow in the minds of the half-informed and of those who wish to be deceived. For a brief moment this chimera looms its huge bulk over serious history; it is pricked; it disappears for ever, carrying with it into the shades the greatest of historians, perhaps the greatest of English prose writers. What do we really know about it?

The first hint of trouble given by the hydrocele occurs in a letter by Gibbon to his friend Lord Sheffield. It is so delicious, so typical of the eighteenth century, of which Gibbon himself was probably the most typical representative, that I cannot resist re-telling it. Two days before, he has hinted to his friend that he was rather unwell; now he modestly draws the veil. "Have you never observed, through my inexpressibles, a large prominency *circa genitalia*, which, as it was not very painful and very little troublesome, I had strangely neglected for many years?" "A large prominency *circa genitalia*" is a variation on the "lump in me privits, doctor," to which we are more accustomed. Gibbon's is the more graceful, and reminds us of the mind which had described chivalry as the "worship of God and the ladies"; the courteous and urbane turn of speech which refuses to call a spade a spade lest some polite ear may be offended.

Gibbon had been staying at Sheffield House in the preceding June—the letter was written in November—and his friends all noted that "Mr. G." had become strangely loath to take exercise and very inert in his movements. Indeed, he had detained the house-party in the house during lovely days together while he had orated to them on the folly of unnecessary exertion; and such was his charm that every one, both women as well as men, seems to have cheerfully given up the glorious English June weather to keep him company. Never was he more brilliant—never a more delightful companion; yet all the time he was like the Spartan boy and the wolf, for he knew of his secret trouble, yet he thought that no one else suspected. It is an instance of how little we see ourselves as others see us that this supremely able man, who could see as far into a millstone as anyone, lived for years with a hydrocele that reached below his knees while he wore the tight breeches of the eighteenth century and was in the fond delusion that nobody else knew anything about it. Of course, everybody knew; probably it had been the cause of secret merriment among all his acquaintance; when the tragedy came to its last act it turned out that every one had been talking about it all the time, and that they had thought it to be a rupture about which Mr. Gibbon had of course taken advice.

After leaving Sheffield House the hydrocele suddenly increased, as Gibbon himself says, "most stupendously"; and it began to dawn upon him that it "ought to be diminished." So he called upon Dr. Walter Farquhar; and Dr. Farquhar was very serious and called in Dr. Cline, "a surgeon of the first eminence," both of whom "viewed it and palped it" and pronounced it a hydrocele. Mr. Gibbon, with his usual good sense and calm mind, prepared to face the necessary "operation" and a future prospect of wearing a truss which Dr. Cline intended to order for him. In the meantime he was to crawl about with some labour and "much indecency," and he prayed Lord Sheffield to "varnish the business to the ladies, yet I am much afraid it will become public," as if anything could any longer conceal the existence of this monstrous chimera. It is hardly credible, but Gibbon had had the hydrocele since 1761—thirty-two years—yet had never even hinted of it to Lord Sheffield, with whom he had probably discussed every other fact connected with his life; and had even forbidden his valet to mention it in his presence or to anyone else. Gibbon, the historian who, more than any other, set Reason and Common Sense on their thrones, seems to have been ashamed of his hydrocele. Once more we wonder how little even able men may perceive the truth of things! In 1761 he had consulted Cæsar Hawkins, who apparently had not been able to make up his mind whether it was a hernia or a hydrocele. In 1787 Lord Sheffield had noticed a sudden great increase in the size of the thing; and in 1793, as we have seen, it came to tragedy.

He was tapped for the hydrocele on November 14; four quarts of fluid were removed, the swelling was diminished to nearly half its size, and the remaining part was a "soft irregular mass." Evidently there was more there than a simple hydrocele, and straightway it began to refill so rapidly that they had to agree to re-tap it in a fortnight. Mr. Cline must have felt anxious; he would know "how many beans make five" well enough, and his patient was the most distinguished man in the world. Many students who have at examinations in clinical surgery wrestled with Cline's splint will probably consider that Cline's punishment for inventing that weapon really began on the day when he perceived Gibbon's hydrocele to be rapidly re-filling. The fortnight passed, and the second tapping took place, "much longer, more searching, and more painful" than before, though only three quarts of fluid were removed; yet Mr. Gibbon said he was much more relieved than by the first attempt. Thence he went to stay with Lord Auckland at a place called Eden Farm; thence again to Sheffield House. There, in the dear house which to him was a home, he was more brilliant than ever before. It was his "swan song." A few days later he was in great pain and moved with difficulty, the swelling again increased enormously, inflammation set in, and he became fevered, and his friends insisted on his return to London. He returned in January, 1794, reaching his chambers after a night of agony in the coach; and Cline again tapped him on January 13. By this time the tumour was enormous, ulcerated and inflamed, and Cline got away six quarts. On January 15 he felt fairly well except for an occasional pain in his stomach, and he told some of his friends that he thought he might probably live for twenty years. That night he had great pain, and got his valet to apply hot napkins to his abdomen; he felt that he wished to vomit. At four in the morning his pain became much easier, and at eight he was able to rise unaided; but by nine he was glad to get back into bed, although he felt, as he said, *plus adroit* than he had felt for months. By eleven he was speechless and obviously dying, and by 1 p.m. he was dead.

I believe that the key to this extraordinary and confused narrative is to be found in the visit to Cæsar Hawkins thirty years before, when that competent surgeon was unable to satisfy himself as to whether he was dealing with a rupture or a hydrocele. It seems now clear that in reality it was both; and Gibbon, who was a corpulent man with a pendulous abdomen, lived for thirty years without taking care of it. But he lived very quietly; he took no exercise; he was a man of calm, placid, and unruffled mind; probably no man was less likely to be incommoded by a hernia, especially if the sac had a large wide mouth and the contents were mainly fat. But the time came when the intra-abdominal pressure of the growing omentum became too great, and the swelling enormously increased, first in 1787 and again in 1793. When Cline first tapped the swelling he was obviously aware that there was more present than a hydrocele, because he warned Gibbon that he would have to wear a truss afterwards, and moreover, though he removed four quarts of fluid, yet the swelling was only reduced by a half. Probably the soft irregular mass which he then left behind was simply omentum which had come down from the abdomen. But why did the swelling begin to grow again immediately? That is not the usual way with a hydrocele, whose growth and everything connected with it are usually indolently leisurely. Could there have been a malignant tumour in course of formation? But if so, would not that have caused more trouble? Nor would it have given the impression of being a soft irregular mass. However, the second tapping was longer and more painful than the first, though it removed less fluid; and Gibbon was more relieved. But this tapping was followed by inflammation. What had happened? Possibly Cline had found the epididymis; more probably his trochar was septic, like all other instruments of that pre-antiseptic period; at all events, the thing went from bad to worse, grew enormously, and severe constitutional symptoms set in. The ulceration and redness of the skin, which was no doubt filthy enough—surgically speaking—after thirty years of hydrocele, look uncommonly like suppurative epididymitis, or suppuration in the hydrocele. Thus Gibbon goes on for a few days, able to move about, though with difficulty, till he cheers up and seems to be recovering; then falls the axe, and he dies a few hours after saying that he thought he had a good chance of living for twenty years.

Could the great septic hydrocele, connected with the abdomen through the inguinal ring, have suddenly burst its bonds and flooded the peritoneum with streptococci? Streptococcic peritonitis is one of the most appalling diseases in surgery. Its symptoms to begin with are vague, and it spreads with the rapidity of a grass fire in summer. After an abdominal section the patient suddenly feels exceedingly weak, there is a little lazy vomiting, the abdomen becomes distended, the pulse goes to pieces in a few hours, and death occurs rapidly while the mind is yet clear. The surgeon usually calls it "shock," or thinks in his own heart that his assistant is a careless fellow; but the real truth is that streptococci have somehow been introduced into the abdomen and have slain the patient without giving time for the formation of adhesions whereby they might have been shut off and ultimately destroyed. That is what I believe happened to Edward Gibbon.

The loss to literature through this untimely tragedy was, of course, irreparable. Gibbon had taken twenty years to mature his unrivalled literary art. His style was the result of unremitting labour and exquisite literary taste; if one accustoms oneself to the constant antitheses—which occasionally give the impression of being forced almost more for the sake of dramatic emphasis than truth—one must be struck with the unvarying majesty and haunting music of the diction, illumined by an irony so sly, so subtle—possibly a trifle malicious—that one simmers with joyous appreciation in the reading. That sort of irony is more appreciated by the onlookers than by its victims, and it is not to be marvelled at that religious people felt deeply aggrieved for many years at the application of it to the Early Christians. Yet, after all, what Gibbon did was nothing more than to show them as men like others; he merely showed that the evidence concerning the beginnings of Christendom was less reliable than the Church had supposed. The *Decline and Fall of the Roman Empire* shows the history of the world for more than a thousand years, so vividly, so dramatically, that the characters—who are great nations—move on the stage like actors, and the men who led them live in a remarkable flood of living light. The general effect upon the reader is as if he were comfortably seated in a moving balloon traversing over Time as over continents; as if he were seated in Mr. Wells's "Time Machine," viewing the disordered beginnings of modern civilization. I believe that no serious flaw in Gibbon's history has been found, from the point of view of accuracy. Some people have found it too much a *chronique scandaleuse*, and some modern historians appear to consider that history should be written in a dull and pedantic style rather than be made to live; furthermore, the great advance in knowledge of the Slavonic peoples has tended to modify some of his conclusions. Nevertheless, Gibbon remains, and so far as we can see, will ever remain, the greatest of historians. Though we might not have had another *Decline and Fall of the Roman Empire,* yet we might reasonably have looked for the completion of that autobiography which had such a brilliant beginning. What would we not give if that cool and appraising mind, which had raised Justinian and Belisarius from the dead and caused them to live again in the hearts of mankind, could have given its impressions of the momentous period in which it came to maturity? If, instead of England receiving its strongest impression of the French Revolution from Carlyle— whose powers of declamation were more potent than his sense of truth—it had been swayed from the beginning by Gibbon? In such a case the history of modern England—possibly of modern Russia—might have been widely different from what we have already seen.

Jean Paul Marat

IT has always been the pride of the medical profession that its aim is to benefit mankind; but opinions may differ as to how far this aim was fulfilled by one of our most eminent confrères, Jean Paul Marat. He was born in Neufchatel of a marriage between a Sardinian man and a Swiss woman, and studied medicine at Bordeaux; thence, after a time at Paris, he went to London, and for some years practised there. In London he published *A Philosophical Essay on Man*, wherein he showed enormous knowledge of the English, German, French, Italian, and Spanish philosophers; and advanced the thesis that a knowledge of science was necessary for eminence as a philosopher. By this essay he fell foul of Voltaire, who answered him tartly that nobody objected to his opinions, but that at least he might learn to express them more politely, especially when dealing with men of greater brains than his own.

The French Revolution was threatening; the coming storm was already thundering, when, in 1788, Marat's ill-balanced mind led him to abandon medicine and take to politics. He returned to Paris, beginning the newspaper *L'Ami du Peuple*, which he continued to edit till late in 1792. His policy was simple, and touched the great heart of the people. "Whatsoever things were pure, whatsoever things were of good repute, whatsoever things were honest"—so be it that they were not Jean Paul Marat's, those things he vilified. He suspected everybody, and constantly cried, "Nous sommes trahis"—that battle-cry of Marat which remained the battle-cry of Paris from that day to 1914. By his violent attacks on every one he made Paris too hot to hold him, and once again retired to London. Later he returned to Paris, apparently at the request of men who desired to use his literary skill and violent doctrines; he had to hide in cellars and sewers, where it was said he contracted that loathsome skin disease which was henceforth to make his life intolerable, and to force him to spend much of his time in a hot-water bath, and would have shortly killed him only for the intervention of Charlotte Corday. In these haunts he was attended only by Simonne Everard, whose loyalty goes to show either that there was some good even in Marat, or that there is no man so frightful but that some woman may be found to love him. Finally, he was elected to the Convention, and took his seat. There he continued his violent attacks upon everybody, urging that the "gangrene" of the aristocracy and bourgeoisie should be amputated from the State. His ideas of political economy appear to have foreshadowed those of Karl Marx—that the proletariat should possess everything, and that nobody else should possess anything. Daily increasing numbers of heads should fall in the sacred names of Liberty, Fraternity, and Equality. At first a mere 600 would have satisfied him, but the number rapidly increased, first to 10,000, then to 260,000. To this number he appeared faithful, for he seldom exceeded it; his most glorious vision was only of killing 300,000 daily.

He devoted his energies to attacking those who appeared abler and better than himself, and the most prominent object of his hatred was the party of the Girondins. These were so called because most of them came from the Gironde, and they are best described as people who wished that France should be governed by a sane and moderate democracy, such as they wrongly imagined the Roman Republic to have been. They were gentle and clever visionaries, who dreamed dreams; they advised, but did not dare to perform; the most famous names which have survived are those of Brissot, Roland, and Barbaroux. Madame Roland, who has become of legendary fame, was considered their "soul"; concerning her, shouts Carlyle: "Radiant with enthusiasm are those dark eyes, is that strong Minerva-face, looking dignity and earnest joy; joyfullest she where all are joyful. Reader, mark that queen-like burgher-woman; beautiful, Amazonian-graceful to the eye; more so to the mind. Unconscious of her worth (as all worth is), of her greatness, of her crystal-clearness, genuine, the creature of Sincerity and Nature, in an age of Artificiality, Pollution and Cant"—and so forth. But Carlyle was writing prose-poetry, sacrificing truth to effect, and it is unwise to take his poetical descriptions as accurate. Recent researches have shown that possibly Manon Roland was not so pure, honest, and well-intentioned as Carlyle thought—nor so "crystal-clear." Summed up, the Girondins represented the middle classes, and the battle was now set between them and the "unwashed," led by Robespierre, Danton, and Marat.

What manner of man, then, was this Marat, physically? Extraordinary! Semi-human from most accounts. Says Carlyle: "O Marat, thou remarkablest horse-leech, once in d'Artois' stable, as thy bleared soul looks forth through thy bleared, dull-acrid, woe-stricken face, what seest thou in all this?" Again: "One most squalidest bleared mortal, redolent of soot and horse-drugs." There appears to have been a certain amount of foundation for the lie that Marat had been nothing more than a horse-doctor, for once when he was brevet-surgeon to the bodyguard of the Compte d'Artois he had found that he could not make a living, and had been driven to dispense medicines for men and horses; his enemies afterwards said that he had never been anything more than a horse-leech. Let us not deprive our own profession of one of its ornaments. His admirer Panis said that while Marat was hiding in the cellars, "he remained for six weeks on one buttock in a dungeon"; immediately, therefore, he was likened to St. Simeon Stylites, who, outside Antioch, built himself a high column, repaired him to the top, and stood there bowing and glorifying God for thirty years, until he became covered with sores. Dr. Moore gives the best description of him. "Marat is a little man of a cadaverous complexion, and countenance exceedingly expressive of his disposition; to a painter of massacres Marat's head would be invaluable. Such heads are rare in this country (England), yet they are sometimes to be met with in the Old Bailey." Marat's head was enormous; he was less than five feet high, with shrivelled limbs and yellow face; one eye was higher placed than the other, "so that he looked lop-sided." As for his skin disease, modern writers seem to consider that we should nowadays call it "dermatitis herpetiformis," though his political friends artlessly thought it was due to the humours generated by excessive patriotism in so small a body attacking his skin, and thus should be counted for a virtue. Carlyle hints that it was syphilis, thus following in the easy track of those who attribute to syphilis those things which they cannot understand. But syphilis, even if painful, would not have been relieved by sitting for hours daily in a hot bath.

Mentally he appears to have been a paranoiac, to quote a recent historical diagnosis by Dr. Charles W. Burr, of Philadelphia. Marat suffered for many years from delusions of persecution, which some people appear to take at their face value; the *New Age Encyclopedia* specially remarks on the amount of persecution that he endured—probably all delusional, unless we are to consider the natural efforts of people in self-defence to be persecution. He suffered from tremendous and persistent "ego-mania," and appears to have believed that he had a greater intellect than Voltaire. Marat, whom the mass of mankind regarded with horror, fancied himself a popular physician, whom crowds would have consulted but for the unreasonable and successful hatred of his enemies. Possibly failure at his profession, combined with the unspeakable irritation of his disease, may have embittered his mind, and for the last few months of his life there can be little doubt that Marat was insane.

It seems to be certain that he organized, if he did not originate, the frightful September massacres. There were many hundreds of Royalists in the prisons, who were becoming a nuisance. The Revolution was hanging fire, and well-meaning enthusiasts began to fear that the dull clod of a populace would not rise in its might to end the aristocracy; so it was decided to abolish these unfortunate prisoners. A tribunal was formed to sit in judgment; outside waited a great crowd of murderers hired for the occasion.

The prisoners were led before the tribunal, and released into the street, where they were received by the murderers and were duly "released"—from this sorrowful world. The most famous victim was the good and gentle Princess de Lamballe, Superintendent of the Queen's Household. The judge at her trial was the notorious Hébert, anarchist, atheist, and savage, afterwards executed by his friend Robespierre when he had served his turn. Madame collapsed with terror, and fainted repeatedly during the mockery of a trial, but when Hébert said the usual ironical, "Let Madame be released," she walked to the door. When she saw the murderers with their bloody swords she shrank back and shrieked, "Fi—horreur." They cut her in pieces; but decency forbids that I should say what they did with all the pieces. Carlyle, who here speaks truth, has a dark saying about "obscene horrors with moustachio *grands-levres*," which is near enough for anatomists to understand. The murderers then stuck her head on a pike, and held her fair curls before the Queen's window as an oriflamme in the name of Liberty. Madame was but one of 1,100 whose insane butchery must be laid to the door of Marat; though some friends of the Bolsheviks endeavour to acquit him we can only say that if it was not his work it looks uncommonly like it.

The battle between the Girondins, who were bad fellows, but less bad than their enemies of the "Mountain"—Robespierre, Danton, and Marat—continued; it was a case of *arcades ambo*, which Bryon translates "blackguards both," though Virgil, who wrote the line—in the Georgics—probably meant something much coarser. The "Mountain" began to get the upper hand, and the Girondins fled for their lives, or went to the guillotine. The Revolution was already "devouring its children."

At Caen in Normandy there lived a young woman, daughter of a decayed noble family which in happier days had been named d'Armont, now Corday. Her name was Marie Charlotte d'Armont, and she is known to history as Charlotte Corday. She had been well educated, had read Rousseau, Voltaire, and the encyclopædists, besides being fascinated by a dream of an imaginary State which she had been taught to call the Roman Republic, in which the "tyrannicide" Brutus loomed much larger and more glorious than in reality. Some Girondists fled to Caen to escape the vengeance of Marat; Charlotte, horrified, resolved that the monster should die; she herself was then nearly twenty-five years of age. I have a picture of her which seems to fit in very well with one's preconceived ideas of her character. She was five feet one inch in height, with a well-proportioned figure, and she had a wonderful mass of chestnut hair; her eyes were large, grey, and set widely apart; the general expression of her face was thoughtful and earnest. Perhaps it would hardly be respectful to call her an "intense" young lady; but there was a young lady who sometimes used to consult me who might very well have sat for the portrait; she possessed a type of somewhat—dare I say?—priggish neurosis which I imagine was not unlike the type of character that dwelt within Charlotte Corday—extreme conscientiousness and self-righteousness. Such a face might have been the face of a Christian martyr going to the lions—if any Christian martyrs were ever thrown to the lions, which some doubt. She went silently to Paris, attended only by an aged man-servant, and bought a long knife in the Palais Royal; thence she went to Marat's house, and tried to procure admission. Simonne—the loyal Simonne—denied her, and she returned to her inn. Again she called at the house; Marat heard her pretty voice, and ordered Simonne to admit her. It was the evening of July 13, four years all but one day since the storming of the Bastille, and Marat sat in his slipper-bath, pens, ink, and paper before him, frightful head peering out of the opening, hot compresses concealing his hair. Charlotte told him that there were several Girondists hiding at Caen and plotting against the Revolution. "Their heads shall fall within a fortnight," croaked Marat. Then, he being thus convicted out of his own mouth, she drew forth from her bosom her long knife, and plunged it into his chest between the first and second ribs, so that it pierced the aorta. Marat gave one cry, and died; Charlotte turned to face the two women who rushed in, but not yet was she to surrender, for she barricaded herself behind some furniture and other movables till the soldiers arrived. To them she gave herself up without trouble.

At her trial she made no denial, but proudly confessed, saying, "Yes, I killed him." Fouquier-Tinville sneered at her: "You must be well practised at this sort of crime!" She only answered: "The monster!—he seems to think I am an assassin!" She thought herself rather the agent of God, sent by Him to rid the world of a loathsome disorder, as Brutus had rid Rome of Julius Cæsar.

In due course she was guillotined, and an extraordinary thing happened. A young German named Adam Lux had been present at the trial, standing behind the artist who was painting the very picture of which I have a reproduction—it is said that Charlotte showed no objection to being portrayed—and the young man had been fascinated by the martyresque air of her. He attended the execution, romance and grief weighing him down; then he ran home, and wrote a furious onslaught on the leaders of the Mountain who had executed her, saying that her death had "sanctified the guillotine," and that it had become "a sacred altar from which every taint had been removed by her innocent blood." He published this broadcast, and was naturally at once arrested. The revolutionary tribunal sentenced him to death, and he scornfully refused to accept a pardon, saying that he wished to die on the same spot as Charlotte, so they let him have his wish. The incident reminds one of a picture-show, and it is not remarkable that an American, named Lyndsay Orr, has written a sentimental article about it.

The people of Paris went mad after Marat's death; his body, which was said to be decaying with unusual rapidity, was surrounded by a great crowd which worshipped it blasphemously, saying, "O Sacred Heart of Marat!" This worship of Marat, which showed how deeply his teaching had bitten into the hearts of the people, culminated in the Reign of Terror, which began on September 5, 1795, whereby France lost, according to different estimates, between half a million and a million innocent people. Some superior persons seem to think that Marat had little or no influence on the Revolution, but to my mind there can be no doubt that the Terror was largely the result of his preaching of frantic violence, and it is a lesson that we ourselves should take to heart, seeing that there are persons in the world to-day who would emulate Marat if they possessed his enormous courage.

I need not narrate the history of the Reign of Terror, which was even worse than the terror which the Bolsheviks established in Russia. Not even Lenin and Trotsky devised anything so atrocious as the *noyades*—wholesale drownings—in the Loire, or the *mariages républicains* on the banks of that river, and it is difficult to believe that the teaching of Marat had nothing to do with that frightful outbreak of bestiality, lust, and murder.

The evil that men do lives after them. There was little good to be buried in Marat's grave, doctor though he was.

Napoleon I

THERE is not, and may possibly never be, an adequate biography of this prodigious man. It is a truism to say that he has cast a doubt on all past glory; let us hope that he has rendered future glory impossible, for to judge by the late war it seems impossible that any rival to the glory of Napoleon can ever arise. In the matter of slaying his fellow-creatures he appears to have reached the summit of human achievement; possibly also in all matters of organization and administration. Material things hardly seemed to affect him; bestriding the world like a colossus he has given us a sublime instance of Intellect that for many years ruthlessly overmastered Circumstance. That Intellect was finally itself mastered by disease, leaving behind it a record which is of supreme interest to mankind; a record which, alas, is so disfigured by prejudice and falsehood that it is difficult to distinguish between what is true and what is untrue. Napoleon himself possessed so extraordinary a personality that nearly every one whom he met became a fervent adorer. With regard to him we can find no half-tones, no detached reporters; therefore it is enormously difficult to find even the basis for a biography. Fortunately, that is not now our province. It is merely necessary that we shall attempt to make a consistent story of the reports of illness which perplex us in regard to his life and death; it adds interest to the quest when we are told that sometimes disease lent its aid to Fate in swaying the destinies of battles. And yet, even after Napoleon has lived, there are some historians who deny the influence of a "great man" upon history, and would attribute to "tendencies" and "ideas" events which ordinary people would attribute to individual genius. Some persons think that Napoleon was merely an episode—that he had no real influence upon history; it is the custom to point to his career as an exemplification of the thesis that war has played very little real part in the moulding of the course of the world. Into all this we need not now enter, beyond saying that he was the "child of the French Revolution" who killed his own spiritual father; the reaction from Napoleon was Metternich, Castlereagh, and the Holy Alliance; the reaction from these forces of repression was the late war. So it is difficult to agree that Napoleon was only an "episode." We have merely to remark that he was the most interesting of all men, and, so far as we can tell, will probably remain so. As Fielding long ago pointed out in *Jonathan Wild*, a man's "greatness" appears to depend on his homicidal capacity. To make yourself a hero all you have to do is to slaughter as many of your fellow-creatures as God will permit. How poor the figures of Woodrow Wilson or Judge Hughes seem beside the grey-coated "little corporal"! Though it is quite probable that either of these most estimable American peacemakers have done more good for the human race than was achieved by any warrior! So sinful is man that we throw our hats in the air and whoop for Napoleon the slaughterer, rather than for Woodrow Wilson, who was "too proud to fight."

When Napoleon was sent to St. Helena he was followed by a very few faithful friends, who seem to have spent their time in hating one another rather than in comforting their fallen idol. It is difficult to get at the truth of these last few years because, though most of the eye-witnesses have published their memoirs, each man seems to have been more concerned to assure the world of the greatness of his own sacrifice than to record the exact facts. Therefore, though Napoleon urged them to keep diaries, and thereby make great sums of money through their imprisonment, yet these diaries generally seem to have aimed rather at attacking the other faithful ones than at telling us exactly what happened.

The post-mortem examination of Napoleon's body was performed by Francesco Antommarchi, a young Corsican physician, anatomist, and pathologist, who was sent to St. Helena about eighteen months before Napoleon's death in the hope that he, being a Corsican, would be able to win the Emperor's confidence and cure the illness of which he was already complaining. Unfortunately, Antommarchi was a very young man, and Napoleon suspected both his medical skill and the reason of his presence. Napoleon used to suffer from severe pains in his stomach; he would clasp himself, and groan, "O, mon pylore!" By that time he was suffering from cancer of the stomach, and Antommarchi did not suspect it. When Napoleon groaned and writhed in agony it is said that Antommarchi merely laughed, and prescribed him tartar emetic in lemonade. Napoleon was violently sick, and thought himself poisoned; he swore he would never again taste any of Antommarchi's medicine. Once again Antommarchi attempted to give him tartar emetic in lemonade; it was not in vain that Napoleon had won a reputation for being a great strategist, for, when Antommarchi's back was turned he handed the draught to the unsuspecting Montholon. In ten minutes that hero reacted in the usual manner, and extremely violently. Napoleon was horrified and outraged in his feelings; quite naturally he accused Antommarchi of trying to poison him, called him "assassin," and refused to see him again. Another fault that Napoleon found with the unhappy young man was that whenever he wanted medical attendance Antommarchi was not to be found, but had to be ferreted out from Jamestown, three and a half miles away; so altogether Antommarchi's attendance could not be called a success. Napoleon in his wrath was "terrible as an army with banners." Even at St. Helena, where the resources of the whole world had been expended in the effort to cage him helpless, it must have been no joke to stand up before those awful eyes, that scorching tongue; and it is no wonder that Antommarchi preferred to spend the last few weeks idling about Jamestown rather than forcing unwelcome attention upon his terrible patient.

Worst of all, Antommarchi at first persuaded himself that Napoleon's last illness was not serious. When Napoleon cried in his agony, "O, mon pylore!" and complained of a pain that shot through him like a knife, Antommarchi merely laughed and turned to his antimony with catastrophic results. It shakes our faith in Antommarchi's professional skill to read that until the very last moment he would not believe that there was much the matter. The veriest blockhead—one would imagine—must have seen that the Emperor was seriously ill. Many a case of cancer of the stomach has been mistaken for simple dyspepsia in its early stages, but there comes a time when the true nature of the disease forces itself upon even the most casual observer. The rapid wasting, the cachexia, the vomiting, the pain, all impress themselves upon both patient and friends, and it is difficult to avoid the conclusion that Antommarchi must have been both careless and negligent. When the inevitable happened, and Napoleon died, it was Antommarchi who performed the autopsy, and found a condition which it is charitable to suppose may have masked the last symptoms and may have explained, if it did not excuse, the young anatomist's mistaken confidence.

We conclude our brief sketch of the unhappy Antommarchi by saying that when he returned to Europe he published the least accurate and most disingenuous of all accounts of Napoleon's last days. His object seems to have been rather to conceal his own shortcomings than to tell the truth. This book sets the seal on his character, and casts doubt on all else that comes from his pen. He may have been, as the *Lancet* says, a "trained and competent pathologist"; he was certainly a most unfortunate young man.

The post-mortem was performed in the presence of several British military surgeons, who appear to have been true sons of John Bull, with all the prejudice, ignorance, and cocksureness that in the eyes of other nations distinguish us so splendidly. Though truthfulness was not a strong point with Antommarchi, he seems to have known his pathology, and has left us an exceedingly good and well-written report of what he found. Strange to relate, the body was found to be still covered thickly with a superficial layer of fat, and the heart and omenta were also adipose. This would seem impossible in the body of a man who had just died from cancer of the stomach, but is corroborated by a report from a Dr. Henry, who was also present, and is not unknown. I remember the case of an old woman who, though hardly at all wasted, was found at the autopsy to have an extensive cancerous growth of the pylorus; the explanation was that the disease had been so acute that it slew her before there had been time to produce much wasting. At one point Napoleon's cancerous ulcer had perforated the stomach, and the orifice had been sealed by adhesions. Dr. Henry proudly states that he himself was able to thrust his finger through it. The liver was large but not diseased; the spleen was large and "full of blood"—probably Antommarchi meant engorged. The intestine was covered by small bright-red patches, evidently showing inflammation of lymphatic tissue such as frequently occurs in general infections of the body. The bladder contained gravel and several definite calculi. There was hardly any secondary cancerous development, except for a few enlarged glands. Antommarchi and the French generally had diagnosed before death that he was suffering from some sort of hepatitis endemic to St. Helena, and the cancer was a great surprise to them—not that it would have mattered much from the point of view of treatment.

Napoleon's hands and feet were extremely small; his skin was white and delicate; his body had feminine characteristics, such as wide hips and narrow shoulders; his reproductive organs were small and apparently atrophied. He is said to have been impotent for some time before he died. There was little hair on the body, and the hair of the head was fine, silky, and sparse. Twenty years later his body was exhumed and taken to France, and Dr. Guillard, who was permitted to make a brief examination, stated that the beard and nails appeared to have grown since death; there was very little sign of decomposition; men who had known him in life recognized his face immediately it was uncovered.

Leonard Guthrie points out that some of these signs seem to indicate a condition of hypo-pituitarism—the opposite to the condition of hyper-pituitarism which causes "giantism." Far-fetched as this theory may appear, yet it is possible that there may be something in it.

The autopsy showed beyond cavil that the cause of death was cancer of the stomach, and it is difficult to see what more Antommarchi could have done in the way of treatment than he did, although certainly an irritant poison like tartar emetic would not have been good for a man with cancer of the stomach, even if it did not actually shorten his life. But Napoleon was not a good patient. He had seen too much of army surgery to have a great respect for our profession; indeed, it is probable that he had no respect for anybody but the Emperor Napoleon. He, at least, knew his business. He could manœuvre a great army in the field and win battles—and lose them too. But even a lost Napoleonic battle—there were not many—was better managed than a victory of any other man; whereas when you were dealing with these doctor fellows you could never tell whether their results were caused by their treatment or by the intervention of whatever gods there be. Decidedly Antommarchi was the last man in the world to be sent to treat the fallen, but still imperious, warrior.

The symptoms of impending death seem to have been masked by a continued fever, and probably Antommarchi was not really much to blame. This idea is to some extent borne out by a couple of specimens in the Museum of the Royal College of Surgeons, which are said to have belonged to the body of Napoleon. The story is that they were surreptitiously removed by Antommarchi, and handed by him to Barry O'Meara, who in his turn gave them to Sir Astley Cooper. That baronet handed them to the museum, where they are now preserved as of doubtful origin. But their genuineness depends upon whether we can believe that Antommarchi would or could have removed them, and whether O'Meara was telling the truth to Sir Astley Cooper. It is doubtful which of the two first-mentioned men is the less credible, and Cooper could not have known how untruthful O'Meara was to show himself, or he would probably not have thought for one moment that the specimens were genuine. O'Meara was a contentious Irishman who, like most other people, had fallen under the sway of Napoleon's personal charm. He published a book in which he libelled Sir Hudson Lowe, whose hard fate it was to be Napoleon's jailer at St. Helena—that isle of unrest. For some reason Lowe never took action against his traducer until it was too late, so that his own character, like most things connected with Napoleon, still remains a bone of contention. But O'Meara had definitely put himself on the side of the French against the English, and it was the object of the French to show that their demigod had died of some illness endemic to that devil's island, aggravated by the barbarous ill-treatment of the brutal British. We on our side contended that St. Helena was a sort of earthly paradise, where one should live for ever. The fragments are from *somebody's* ileum, and show little raised patches of inflamed lymphoid tissue; Sir William Leishman considers the post-mortem findings, apart from the cancer, those of some long-continued fever, such as Mediterranean fever.

Mediterranean or Malta fever is a curious specific fever due to the *Micrococcus melitensis*, which shows itself by recurrent bouts of pyrexia, accompanied by constipation, chronic anæmia, and wasting. Between the bouts the patient may appear perfectly well. There are three types—the "undulatory" here described; the "intermittent," in which the attacks come on almost daily; and the "malignant," in which the patient only lives for a week or ten days. It is now known to be contracted by drinking the infected milk of goats, and it is almost confined to the shores of the Mediterranean and certain parts of India. It may last for years, and it is quite possible that Napoleon caught it at Elba, of which Mediterranean island he was the unwilling emperor in 1814. Thence he returned to France, as it was said, because he had not elba-room on his little kingdom. It is certain that for years he had been subject to feverish attacks, which army surgeons would now possibly classify as "P.U.O.," and it is quite possible that these may in reality have been manifestations of Malta fever.

It has been surmised by some enthusiasts that the frequency of micturition, followed by dysuria, to which he was liable, may have really been due to hyper-pituitarism. Whenever we do not understand a thing let us blame a ductless gland; the pituitary body is well hidden beneath the brain, and its action is still not thoroughly understood. But surely we need no further explanation of this miserable symptom than the stones in the bladder. Napoleon for many years might almost be said to have lived on horseback, and riding is the very thing to cause untold misery to a man afflicted with vesical calculus. Dysuria, attendant upon frequency of micturition, is a most suggestive symptom; nowadays we are always taught to consider the possibility of stone, and it is rather surprising that nobody seems to have suspected it during his lifetime. This could be very well accounted for by remembering the general ignorance and incompetence of army surgeons at the time, the mighty position of the patient, and his intolerance of the medical profession. Few men would have dared to suggest that it would be well for him to submit to the passage of a sound, even if the trouble ever became sufficiently urgent to compel him to confide so private a matter to one so lowly as a mere army doctor. Yet he had known and admired Baron Larrey, the great military surgeon of the Napoleonic Wars; one can only surmise that his calculi did not give him much trouble, or that they grew more rapidly in the sedentary life which he had led at St. Helena.

During the last year or so he took great interest in gardening, and spent hours in planting trees, digging the soil, and generally behaving somewhat after the manner of a suburban householder. He was intensely bored by his forced inaction, and used to take refuge in chess. His staff at first welcomed this, but unhappily they could find nobody bad enough for the mighty strategist to beat; yet nobody dared to give him checkmate, and it was necessary to lose the game foolishly rather than to defeat Napoleon. It is clear that the qualities requisite in a good chess-player are by no means the same as those necessary to outmanœuvre an army.

Throughout his life his pulse-rate seldom exceeded fifty per minute; as he grew older he was subject to increasing lassitude; his extremities felt constantly chilly, and he used to lie for hours daily in hot-water baths. Possibly these may have been symptoms of hypo-pituitarism; Lord Rosebery follows popular opinion in attributing his laziness to the weakening effects of hot baths. Occasionally Napoleon suffered from attacks of vomiting, followed by fits of extreme lethargy. It is quite possible that these vomiting attacks may have been due to the gastric ulcer, which must have been growing for years until, about September, 1820, it became acutely malignant.

The legend that Napoleon suffered from epilepsy appears, according to Dr. Ireland, to rest upon a statement in Talleyrand's memoirs. In September, 1805, in Talleyrand's presence, Napoleon was seized after dinner with a sort of fit, and fell to the ground struggling convulsively. Talleyrand loosened his cravat, obeying the popular rule in such circumstances to "give him air." Remusat, the chief chamberlain, gave him water, which he drank. Talleyrand returned to the charge, and "inundated" him with eau-de-Cologne. The Emperor awakened, and said something—one would like to know what he said when he felt the inundation streaming down his clothes—probably something truly of the camp. Half an hour later he was on the road that was to lead him—to Austerlitz, of all places! Clearly this fit, whatever it may have been, was not epilepsy in the ordinary sense of the term. There was no "cry," no biting of the tongue, no foaming at the mouth, and apparently no unconsciousness. Moreover, epilepsy is accompanied by degeneration of the intellect, and nobody dares to say that Austerlitz, Jena, and Wagram— to say nothing of Aspern and Eckmuhl—were won by a degenerate. Eylau and Friedland were also to come after 1805, and these seven names still ring like a trumpet for sheer glory, daring, and supreme genius. I suppose there is not one of them—except perhaps Aspern—which would not have made an imperishable name for any lesser general. It is impossible to believe that they were fought by an epileptic. If Napoleon really had epilepsy it was assuredly not the "*grand mal*" which helps to fill our asylums. It is just possible that "*petit mal*" may have been in the picture. This is a curious condition which manifests itself by momentary loss of consciousness; the patient may become suddenly dreamy and purposeless, and may perform curious involuntary actions—even crimes—while *apparently* conscious. When he recovers he knows nothing about what he has been doing, and may even resume the interrupted action which had occupied him at the moment of the seizure. Some such explanation may account for Napoleon's fits of furious passion, that seem to have been followed by periods of lethargy and vomiting. It is a sort of pleasing paradox—and mankind dearly loves paradox—to say that supremely great men suffer from epilepsy. It was said of Julius Cæsar, of St. Paul, and of Mohammed. These men are said to have suffered from "falling sickness," whatever that may have been; there are plenty of conditions which may make men fall to the ground, without being epileptic: Ménière's disease, for instance. It is ridiculous to suppose that Julius Cæsar and Napoleon—by common consent the two greatest of the sons of men—should have been subject to a disease which deteriorates the intellect.

It is possible that some such trouble as *"petit mal"* may have been at the bottom of the curious stories of a certain listless torpor that appears to have overcome Napoleon at critical moments in his later battles. Something of the kind happened at Borodino in 1812, the bloodiest and most frightful battle in history till that time. Napoleon indeed won, in the sense that the exhausted Russians retreated to Moscow, whither he pursued them to his ill-fortune; but the battle was not fought with anything like the supreme genius which he displayed in his other campaigns. Similarly, he is said to have been thus stricken helpless after Ligny, when he defeated Blucher in 1815. He wasted precious hours in lethargy, which should have been spent in his usual furious pursuit of his beaten foe. To this day the French hold that, but for Napoleon's inexplicable idleness after Ligny, there would have been no St. Helena; and, with all the respect due to Wellington and his thin red line, it is by no means certain that the French are wrong. But nations will continue to squabble about Waterloo till there shall be no more war; and 1814 had been the most brilliant of his campaigns—probably of any man's campaigns.

"Of woman came the beginning of sin, and through her therefore we all die," said the ungallant author of Ecclesiasticus; and it is certain that Napoleon was extremely susceptible to feminine charms. Like a Roman emperor, he had but to cast a glance at a woman and she was at his feet. Yet probably his life was not very much less moral than was customary among the great at that time. When we remember his extraordinary personal charm, it is rather a matter for wonder that women seem to have had so little serious effect upon his life, and he seems to have taken comparatively little advantage of his opportunities. His first wife, Josephine Beauharnais, was a flighty Creole who pleased herself entirely; in the vulgar phrase, she "took her pleasure where she found it." To this Napoleon appears to have been complaisant, but as she could not produce an heir to the dynasty which he wished to found, he divorced her, and married the Austrian princess Marie Louise, whose father he had defeated and humiliated as few sovereigns have ever been humiliated. She deserted him without a qualm when he was sent to Elba; when he was finally imprisoned at St. Helena there was no question of her following him, even if the British Government had had sufficient imagination to permit such a thing. Napoleon, who was fond of her, wanted her to go with him; but one could not expect a Government containing Castlereagh, Liverpool, and Bathurst, to show any sympathy to the fallen foe who had been a nightmare to Europe for twenty years. She would never consent to see Josephine. It is said that Napoleon's *libido sexualis* was violent, but rapidly quelled. In conversation at St. Helena he admitted having possessed seven mistresses; of them he said simply, "C'est beaucoup." When he was sent to St. Helena his mother wrote and asked to be allowed to follow him; however great a man's fall, his mother never deserts him, and asylum doctors find that long after the wife or sisters forget some demented and bestial creature, his mother loyally continues her visits till the grave closes over one or the other. But more remarkable is the fact that Pauline Bonaparte, who was always looked upon as a shameless hussy, would have followed him to St. Helena, only that she was ill in bed at the time. She was the beautiful sister who sat to Canova for the statue of Venus in the Villa Borghese. It was then thought most shocking for a lady of high degree to be sculptured as a nude Venus—perhaps it is now; I say, *perhaps*. There are few ladies of high degree so beautiful as Princess Pauline, as Canova shows her. A friend said to her about the statue, "Were you not uncomfortable, princess, sitting there without any clothes on?" "Uncomfortable," said Princess Pauline, "why should I be uncomfortable? There was a stove in the room!" There are many other still less creditable stories told about her. It was poor beautiful Pauline who lost her husband of yellow fever, herself recovering of an attack at the same time. She cut off her hair and buried it in his coffin. This was thought a wonderful instance of wifely devotion, until the cynical Emperor remarked: "Quite so; quite so; of course, she knows it will grow again better than ever for cutting it off, and that it would have fallen off anyhow after the fever." Yet when he was sent to Elba, this frivolous sister followed him, and she sold every jewel she possessed to make life comfortable for him at St. Helena. She was a very human and beautiful woman, this Pauline; she detested Marie Louise, and once in 1810 at a grand fête she saucily poked out her tongue at the young Empress in full view of all the nobles. Unhappily Napoleon saw her, and cast upon her a dreadful look; Pauline picked up her skirts and ran headlong from the room. When she heard of his death she wept bitterly; she died four years afterwards of cancer. Her last action was to call for a mirror, looking into which she died, saying, "I am still beautiful; I am not afraid to die."

In attempting to judge Marie Louise it must be remembered that there is a horrid story told of Napoleon's first meeting with her in France after the civil marriage had been performed by proxy in Vienna. It is said that the fury of his lust did her physical injury, and that that is the true reason why she never forgave him and deserted him at the first opportunity. She bore him a son, of whom he was passionately fond, but after his downfall the son—the poor little King of Rome immortalized by Rostand in *"l'Aiglon"*—fell into the hands of Metternich, the Austrian, who is said to have deliberately contrived to have him taught improper practices, lest he should grow up to be as terrible a menace to the world as his father. But all these are rumours, and show how difficult it is to ascertain the truth of anything connected with Napoleon.

When Napoleon fell to the dust after Leipzig, Marie Louise became too friendly with Count von Neipperg, whom she morganatically married after Napoleon's death. Although he heard of her infidelity, he forgave her, and mentioned her affectionately in his will, thereby showing, to borrow a famous phrase of Gibbon about Belisarius, "Either less or more than the character of a man."

For nine days before he died he lay unconscious and babbled in delirium. On the morning of May 5, 1821, Montholon thought he heard the words "France ... armée ... tête d'armée." The dying Emperor thrust Montholon from his side, struggled out of bed, and staggered towards the window. Montholon overpowered him and put him back to bed, where he lay silent and motionless till he died the same evening. The man who had fought about sixty pitched battles, all of which he had won, I believe, but two—who had caused the deaths of three millions of his own men and untold millions of his enemies—died as peacefully in his bed as any humble labourer. What dim memories passed through his clouded brain as he tried to say "head of the army"? A great tropical storm was threatening Longwood. Did he recall the famous "sun of Austerlitz" beneath whose rays the grande armée had elevated its idolized head to the highest pitch of earthly glory? Who can follow the queer paths taken by associated ideas in the human brain?

Benvenuto Cellini

NO one can read Benvenuto's extraordinary autobiography without being reminded of the even more extraordinary diary of Mr. Pepys. But there is one very great difference. Cellini dictated his memoirs to a little boy for the world at large, and did not profess to tell the whole truth—rather those things which came into his mind readily in his old age; but Pepys wrote for himself in secret cypher in his own study, and the reason of his writing has never yet been guessed. Why did he set down all his most private affairs? And when they became too disgraceful even for Mr. Pepys's conscience, why did he set them down in a mongrel mixture of French and Spanish? Can we find a hint in the fact that he left a key to the cypher behind him? Did he really wish his Diary to remain unreadable for ever? Was it really a quaint and beastly vanity that moved him?

But Cellini wrote *per medium* of a little boy amanuensis while he himself worked, and possibly he may have deliberately omitted some facts too shameful for the ears of that *puer ingenuus*; though I have my doubts about this theory. He frankly depicts himself as a cynical and forth-right fellow always ready to brawl; untroubled by conventional ideas either of art or of morality; ready to call a spade a spade or any number of adjectived shovels that came instantly to his mind. If it be great writing to express one's meaning tersely, directly, and positively, then Cellini's is the greatest of writing, though we have to be thankful that it is in a foreign language. The best translation is probably that of John Addington Symonds—a cheaper and excellent edition is published in the *Everyman Library*—and nobody who wishes to write precisely as he thinks can afford to go without studying this remarkable book. And having studied it he will probably come to the conclusion that there are other things in writing than merely to express oneself directly. There is such a thing as beauty of thought as well as beauty of expression; and probably he will end by wondering what is that thing which we call beauty? Is it only Truth, as even such a master of Beauty as Keats seems to have thought? Why is one line of the *Grecian Urn* more beautiful than all the blood and thunder of Benvenuto?

Cellini says that he caught the "French evil"—i.e. syphilis—when he was a young man; he certainly did his best to catch it. His symptoms were abnormal, and the doctors assured him that his disease was not the "French evil." However, he knew better, and assumed a treatment of his own, consisting of *lignum vitæ* and a holiday shooting in the marshes. Here he probably caught malaria, of which he cured himself with guaiacum. We know now that, alas, syphilis cannot be cured by such means; and the fact that he lived to old age seems to show that there was something wrong with his diagnosis. I have known plenty of syphilitics who have reached extreme old age, but they had not been cured by *lignum vitæ* and a holiday; it was mercury that had cured them, taken early and often, over long periods. I very much doubt whether he ever had the "French evil" at all.

But apart from this and from his amazing revelations of quarrelling and loose living, the autobiography is worth reading for its remarkable description of the casting of his great statue of Perseus, which now stands in the Loggia dei Lanzi at Florence hard by the Uffizi. By the time the book had reached so far the little boy had long wearied of the job of secretary, and the old man had buckled down to the labour of writing with his own hand. I dare swear that he wrote this particular section at one breath, so to speak; the torrent of words, poured forth in wild excitement, carry the reader away with the frenzy of the writer as Benvenuto recalls the greatest hours of his life. Nowhere is such an instance of the terrible labour pains of a true artist as his offspring comes to birth.

The great statue does more than represent Perseus; it represents the wild and headlong mind of Benvenuto himself. Perseus stands in triumph with the Gorgon's head in one hand and a sword in the other. You can buy paper-knives modelled on this sword for five lire in Florence to-day. The gladness and youthful joy of Perseus are even more striking than those of Verrochio's David in the Bargello just near at hand. Verrochio has modelled a young rascal of a Jew who is clearly saying: "Alone I did it; and very nice too!" Never was boyish triumph better portrayed. But Benvenuto's Perseus is a great young man who has done something very worthy, and knows that it is worthy. He has begun to amputate the head very carefully with a neat circular incision round the neck; then, his rage or his fear of the basilisk glance getting the better of him, he has set his foot against the Gorgon's shoulder and tugged at the head violently until the grisly thing has come away in his hand, tearing through the soft parts of the neck and wrenching the great vessels from the heart.

As is well known, opportunities for performing decapitation upon a Gorgon are few; apart from the rarity of the monster there is always the risk lest the surgeon may be frozen stiff in the midst of the operation; and it becomes still more difficult when it has to be performed in the Fourth Dimension through a looking-glass. We have the authority of *The Mikado* that self-decapitation is a difficult, not to say painful, operation, and Benvenuto could not have practised his method before a shaving-mirror, because he had a bushy beard, though some of us have inadvertently tried in our extreme youth before we have learned the advisability of using safety razors. Anyhow, Benvenuto's Perseus is a very realistic, violent, and wonderful piece of sculpture; if he had done nothing else he would have still been one of the greatest artists in the world. My own misfortune was in going to Florence before I had seriously read his autobiography; I wish to warn others lest that misfortune should befall them. Read Cellini's autobiography—*then*, go to Florence! You will see how the author of the autobiography was the only man who could possibly have done the Perseus; how, in modelling the old pre-hellenic demigod, he was really modelling his own subconscious mind.

Death

WHEN William Dunbar sang, "Timor mortis perturbat me," he but expressed the most universal of human—perhaps of animate—feelings. It is no shame to fear death; the fear appears to be a necessary condition of our existence. The shame begins when we allow that fear to influence us in the performance of our duty. But why should we fear death at all? It is hardly an explanation to say that the fear of death is implanted in living things lest the individual should be too easily slain and thereby the species become extinct. Who implanted it? And why is it so necessary that that individual should survive? Why is it necessary that the species should survive? And so on—to name only a few of the unanswerable questions that crowd upon us whenever we sit down to muse upon that problem which every living thing must some time have a chance of solving. The question of death is inextricably bound up with the interpretation of innumerable abstract nouns, such as truth, justice, good, evil, and many more, which all religions make some effort to interpret. Philosophy attempts it by the light of man's reason; religion by a light from some extra-human source; but all alike represent the struggles of earnest men to solve the insoluble.

Nor is it possible to obtain help from the great men of the past, because not one of them knew any more about death than you do yourself. Socrates, in Plato's *Phædo*, Sir Thomas Browne in the *Religio Medici* and the *Hydriotaphia*, Shakespeare in *Hamlet* and *Macbeth* and many other plays, St. Paul in various epistles, all tried to console us for the fact that we must die; the revolt against that inevitable end of beauty and ugliness, charm and horror, love and hate, is the most persistent note in literature; and there are few men who go through life without permitting themselves to wonder, "What is going to happen to me? Why should I have to die? What will my wife and children do after me? How is it possible that the world will go on, and apparently go on just the same as now, for ages after an important thing like me is shovelled away into a hole in the ground?" I suppose you have dreamed with a start of horror a dream in which you revisit the world, and looking for your own house and children, find them going along happily and apparently prosperous, the milkman coming as usual, a woman in the form of your wife ordering meals and supervising household affairs, the tax-gatherer calling—let us hope a little less often than when you were alive—the trams running and the ferry-boats packed as usual, and the sun shining, the rain falling sometimes, Members of Parliament bawling foolishly over nothing—all these things happening as usual; but you look around to see anybody resembling that beautiful and god-like creature whom you remember as yourself, and wheresoever you look he is not there. Where is he? How can the world possibly go on without him? Is it really going on, or is it nothing more than an incredible dream? And why are you so shocked and horror-stricken by this dream? You could hardly be more shocked if you saw you wife toiling in a garret for the minimum wage, or your children running about barefoot selling newspapers. The shocking fact is not that you have left them penniless, but that you have had to leave them at all. In the morning joy cometh as usual, and you go cheerfully about your work, which simply consists of postponing the day of somebody else's death as long as you can. For a little time perhaps you will take particular note of the facts which accompany the act of death; then you will resign yourself to the inevitable, and continue doggedly to wage an endless battle in which you must inevitably lose, assured of nothing but that some day you too will lie pallid, your jaw dropped, your chest not moving, your face horribly inert; and that somebody will come and wash your body and tie up your jaw and put pennies on your eyes and wrap you in cerements and lift you into a long box; and that large men will put the box on their shoulders and lump you into a big vehicle with black horses, and another man will ironically shout Paul's words, "O death, where is thy sting? O grave, where is thy victory?" And in the club some man will take your seat at lunch, and the others will say you were a decent sort of fellow and will not joke loudly for a whole meal-time. And ten years hence who will remember you? Your wife and children, of course—if they too have not also been carried away in long boxes; a few men who look upon you with a kindly patronage as one who has fallen in the fight and cannot compete with them now; but otherwise? Your hospital appointments have long been filled up by men who cannot, you think, do your work half so well as you used to do it; your car is long ago turned into scrap-iron; your little dog, which used to yelp so joyously when you got home tired at night and kicked him out of the way, is long dead and buried under your favourite rose-bush; your library, which was your joy for so many years, has long been sold at about one-tenth of what it cost you; and, except for the woman who was foolish enough to love and marry you and the children whom the good creature brought into the world to carry on your name, you are as though you had never been. Why should this be? And why are you so terrified at the prospect?

During the past few years we have had ample experience of death, for there are few families in Australia, and I suppose in England, France, Germany, Italy, Russia, and Europe generally, which have not lost some beloved member; yet we are no nearer solving the mystery than we were before. We know no more about it than did Socrates or Homer. The only thing that is beginning to haunt the minds of many men is whether those gallant boys who died in the war were not better off than the men who survived. At least they know the worst, if there be anything to know; and have no longer to fear cancer and paralysis and the other diseases of later life. Many men have written in a consolatory vein about old age, but the consolants have in no way answered the dictum that if by reason of strength our years exceed threescore and ten, yet is our strength but labour and sorrow. No doctor who has seen an old man with an enlarged prostate and a septic kidney therefrom, or with cancer of the tongue, can refrain from wishing that that man had died twenty years sooner, because however bad the fate in store for him it can hardly be worse than what he suffers here on earth. And possibly there are worse things on earth even than cancer of the tongue; possibly cancer of the bladder is the most atrocious, or right-sided hemiplegia with its aphasia and deadly depression of soul. Young men do not suffer from these things; and no one can attend a man so afflicted without wishing that the patient had died happily by a bullet in Gallipoli before his time came so to suffer. Yet as a man grows older, though the likelihood of his death becomes more and more with every passing year, his clinging to bare life, however painful and terrible that life may be, becomes more intense. The young hardly seem to fear death; that is a fear almost confined to the aged. How otherwise can we explain the extraordinary heroism shown by the boys of every army during the late war? I watched many beautiful and gallant boys, volunteers mark you, march down the streets of Sydney on their way to a quarrel which nobody understood—not even the German Kaiser who started it; and when my own turn came to go I patched up many thousands who had been shattered: the one impression made upon me was the utter vileness and beastliness of war, and the glorious courage of the boys in the line. Before the order went forth forbidding the use of Liston's long splint in the advanced dressing stations, men with shattered lower limbs used to be brought in with their feet turned back to front. High-explosive shells would tear away half the front of a man's abdomen; men would be maimed horribly for life, and life would never be the same again for them. Yet none seemed to complain. I know that our own boys simply accepted it all as the inevitable consequence of war, and from what I saw of the English and French their attitude of mind was much the same. The courage of the boys was amazing. I am very sure that if the average age of the armies had been sixty instead of under thirty, Amiens would never have been saved or Fort Douaumont recovered, nor would the Germans have fought so heroically as we must admit they did. Old men feel death approaching them, and they fear it. We all know that our old patients are far more nervous about death than the young. I remember a girl who had sarcoma of the thigh, which recurred after amputation, and I had to send her to a home for the dying. She did not seem very much perturbed. I suppose the proper thing to say would be that she was conscious of her salvation and had nothing to fear; but the truth was that she was a young rake who had committed nearly every crime possible to the female sex, and she died as peacefully and happily as any young member of the Church I ever knew. But who is so terrified as the old woman who trips on a rough edge of the carpet and fractures her thigh-bone? How she clings to life! What terrors attend her last few weeks on earth, till merciful pneumonia comes to send her to endless sleep!

I do not remember to have noticed any of that ecstasy which we are told should attend the dying of the saved. Generally, so far as I have observed, the dying man falls asleep some hours or days before he actually dies, and does not wake again. His breathing becomes more and more feeble; his heart beats more irregularly and feebly, and finally it does not resume; there comes a moment when his face alters indescribably and his jaw drops; one touches his eyes and they do not respond; one holds a mirror to his mouth and it is not dulled; his wife, kneeling by the bedside, suddenly perceives that she is a widow, and cries inconsolably; one turns away sore and grieved and defeated; and that is all about it! There is no more heroism nor pain nor agony in dying than in falling asleep every night. Whether a man has been a good man or a bad does not seem to make any difference. I have seldom seen a death-agony, nor heard a death-rattle that could be distinguished from a commonplace snore. Possibly the muscles may become wanting in oxygenation for some time before actual death, and thrown into convulsive movements like the dance of the highwayman at Tyburn while he was dying of strangulation, and these convulsive movements might be looked upon as a death-agony; but I am quite sure that the patient never feels them. To do so would require that the sense of self-location would persist, but what evidence we have is that that is one of the first senses to depart. Possibly the dying man may have some sensation such as we have all gone through while falling asleep—that feeling as though we are falling, which is supposed to be a survival from the days when we were apes; possibly there may be some giddiness such as attends the going under an anæsthetic, and is doubtless to be attributed to the same loss of power of self-location; but the impression that has been forced upon me whenever I have seen any struggling has been that the movements were quite involuntary, purposeless, and meaningless.

And anything like an agony or a death-rattle is rare. Far more often the man simply falls asleep, and it may be as difficult to decide when life passes into death as it is to decide when consciousness passes into sleep.

Nor have I ever heard any genuine last words such as we read in books. I doubt if they ever occur. At the actual time of death the man's body is far too busy with its dying for his mind to formulate any ideas. The nearest approach to a "last word" that I ever remember was when a very old and brilliant man, who, after a lifetime spent in the service of Australia, lay dying, full of years and honour, from suppression of urine that followed some weeks after an operation on his prostate. It was early in the war, and Austria, with her usual folly, was acting egregiously. The nurse was trying to rouse the old man by reading to him the war news. He suddenly sat up, and a flash of intelligence came over his face. "Pah—Austria with her idiot Archdukes—that was what Bismarck said, wasn't it?" Then he fell back, and went to sleep; nor could the visits of his family and the injections of saline solution into his veins rouse him again from his torpor. He lay unconscious for nearly a week. That is the only instance of the "ruling passion strong in death" that I remember. He had always hated Bismarck and despised the Austrians, and for one brief moment hatred and contempt awakened his clouded brain. And Napoleon said, "Tête d'armée."

There is no need, so far as we can tell, to fear the actual dying. Death is no more to be feared than his twin-brother Sleep, as the very ancient Greeks of Homer surmised; it is *what comes after* that many people fear. "To sleep— perchance to dream" nightmares? Well, I do not know what other people feel when they dream, but for myself I am fortunate enough to know, even in the midst of the most horrible nightmare, that it is all a dream; and I dare say that this is a privilege common to many people. The blessed sleep that comes to tired man in the early morning, with which cometh joy, is well worth going through nightmare to attain; and I think I am not speaking wildly in claiming that most men pass the happiest portions of their lives in that early morning sleep. One of the horrors of neurasthenia is that early morning sleep is often denied to the patient.

But the idea of hell is to many persons a real terror, not to be overmastered by reason. God has not made man in His own image; man has made God in his. As Grant Allen used to say: "The Englishman's idea of God is an Englishman twelve feet high"; and the old Jews, who were a very savage and ruthless people, created Jehovah in their own image. To such a God eternal punishment for a point of belief was quite the natural thing, and nineteen centuries of belief in the teaching of a loving and forgiving Christ have not abolished that frightful idea. It is one of the disservices of the Mediæval Church to mankind that it popularized and enforced the idea of hell, and that idea has been diligently perpetuated by some narrow-minded sects to this very day. But to a modern man, who, with all his faults, is a kindly and forgiving creature, hell is unthinkable, and he cannot bring himself to believe that it was actually part of the teaching of Christ. If the New Testament says so, then, thinks the average modern man, it must be in an interpolation by some mediæval ecclesiastic whose zeal outran his mercy; and an average modern man is not seriously swayed by any idea of everlasting flames. He may even quaintly wonder, if he has studied the known facts of the universe, where either hell or heaven is to be found, considering that they are supposed to have lasted for ever and to be fated to last as long. In time to come the souls, saved and lost, must be of infinite number, if they are not so already; and an infinite number would fill all available space and spill over for an infinite distance, leaving no room for flames, or brimstone, or harps, or golden cities. Perhaps it may not be beyond Almighty Power to solve this difficulty, but it is a very real one to the average thoughtful man. When we begin to realize infinity, to realize that every one of the millions of known suns must each last for millions of years, after which the whole process must begin again, endure as long, and so on *ad infinitum*, the thing becomes simply inconceivable; the mind staggers, and takes refuge in agnosticism, which is not cured by the scoffing of clergymen whom one suspects of not viewing things from a modern standpoint. Jowett once answered a young man whom he evidently looked upon as a "puppy" by thundering at him: "Young man, you call yourself an agnostic; let me tell you that *agnostic* is a Greek word the Latin of which is *ignoramus*!" Jowett evidently did not in the least understand that young man's difficulties, nor the difficulties of any man whose training has been scientific—that is, directed towards the ascertaining what is demonstrably true. Scoffing and insolence like that only react upon the scoffer's head, and rather breed contempt than comfort. Nor is the problem of God Himself any more easy of solution, unless we are prepared to see Him everywhere, in every minute cell and tiny bacterium. If we confess to such a belief we are immediately crushed with the cry of "mere Pantheism," or even "Spinozism," as though these epithets, meant to be contemptuous, led us any further on our way. You cannot solve these dreadful problems by a sneer, and Voltaire, the prince of scoffers, would have had even more influence on thought than he had if he had contented himself with a less aggressive and polemic attitude towards the Church.

Hell is a concrete attempt at Divine punishment. Punishment for what? For disobeying the commandments of God? How are we to know what God really commanded? And how are we to weigh the relative effects of temptation and powers of resistance upon any given man? How are we to say that an action which in one man may be desperately wicked may not be positively virtuous in another? It is a commonplace that virtue changes with latitude, and that we find "the crimes of Clapham chaste in Martaban." Why should we condemn some poor maiden of Clapham to burn for ever for a crime which she may not recognize as a crime, whereas we applaud a damsel of Martaban for doing precisely the same thing? And what is sin? Is there any real evidence as to what the commandments of God really are? Modern psychology seems to hold that virtue and vice are simply phases of the herd-complex of normal man, and have been evolved by the herd during countless generations as the best method of perpetuating the human species. No individual man made his own herd-complex, by which he is so enormously swayed; no individual man made his own sex-complex, or his ego-complex, or anything that is his. How can he be held responsible for his actions by a God Who made him the subject of such frightful temptations and gave him such feeble powers of resistance? Edward Fitzgerald— who, be it remembered, knew no more about these things than you or I— summed up the whole matter in "Man's forgiveness give—and take," and probably this simple line has given more comfort to thoughtful men than all Jowett's bluster. Fitzgerald has at least voiced the instinctive rebellion which every man must feel when he considers the facts of human nature, even if he has given us otherwise no more guidance than a call to a poor kind of Epicureanism which lays stress on a book of verse underneath a bough, and thou beside me singing in a wilderness. If our musings lead us to Epicureanism, at least let it be the Epicureanism of Epicurus, and not the sensual pleasure-seeking of Omar. True, Epicureanism laid stress on the superiority of mental over physical happiness; it were better to worship at the shrine of Beethoven than of Venus, and better to take your pleasure in the library than in the wine-shop. But nobler than Epicurus was Zeno, the Stoic, whose influence on both the ancient and the modern worlds has been so profound. If we are to take philosophy as our guide, Stoicism, which inculcates duty and self-restraint, and is supported by the great names of Seneca, Epictetus, and Marcus Aurelius, is probably our best leading light. Theoretically it should produce noble characters; practically it has produced the noblest, if the *Meditations* of Marcus Aurelius were really written by him and not by some monk in the Middle Ages. If we follow the teaching of Stoicism we shall, when we come to die, at least have the consolation that we have done our duty; and if we realize the full meaning of "duty" in the modern world to include duty done kindly and generously as well as faithfully, we shall be living as nearly to the ideals laid down by Christ as is possible to human nature, and we shall assuredly have nothing to fear.

Anæsthesia gives some faint hint as to the possibility of a future life. It is believed that chloroform and ether abolish consciousness by causing a slight change in the molecular constitution of nervous matter, as for instance dissolving the fatty substances or lipoids. If so minute a change in the chemistry of nervous matter has the power of totally abolishing consciousness, how can the mind possibly survive the much greater change which occurs in nervous matter after corruption has set in? Nor has there ever been any proof that there can be consciousness without living nervous matter. One turns to the spiritualistic evidence offered by Myers, Conan Doyle, Oliver Lodge, and other observers, but after carefully studying their reports one feels inclined to agree with Huxley that spiritualism has merely added a new terror to death, for, according to the spiritualists, death appears to transform men into idiots who on earth were known to be able and clever, and the marvel is not the miracles which they report, but that clever men should be found to believe them.

An even more remarkable marvel than the marvel of Lodge and Conan Doyle was the marvel of John Henry Newman, who, a supremely able man, living at the time of Darwin, Huxley, and the vast biological advancement of the Victorian era, was yet able in middle life to embrace the far from rationalistic doctrines of the Roman Catholic Church. That he was tempted to do so by the opportunity which his action gave him of becoming a prince of the Church is too ridiculous an assumption to stand for a moment. The man *believed* these things, and believed them with greatness, nobility, and earnestness; when he 'verted he was forty-four years of age, and it was not for about thirty years that he was created a cardinal. The only explanation that can be given is that we have not yet fathomed the depths of the human mind; there is a certain type of mind which appears to see things by what it calls intuition and is not open to reason on the basis of evidence or probability.

Probably what most men fear is not death but the pain and illness which generally precede death; and apart from that very natural dread there is the dread of leaving things which are dear to every one. After all, life is sweet to most of us; it is pleasant to feel the warm sun and see the blue sky and watch the shadows race over far hills; an occasional concert, a week-end spent at golf, or at working diligently in the garden; congenial employment, or a worthy book to read, all help to make life worth living, and the mind becomes sad at the thought of leaving these things and the home which they epitomize. I remember once in a troopship, a few days out from an Australian port, when the men had all got over their sea-sickness and were beginning to realize that they really were started on their Great Adventure, that I went down into their quarters at night, and found a big young countryman who had enlisted in the Artillery, sobbing bitterly. It was a long time before kindly consolation and a dose of bromide sent him off to sleep. In the morning he came to see me and tried to apologize for his unmanliness. "I'm not afraid of dyin', sir," he explained. "I want to stoush some of them Germans first, though. It's leaving all me life in Australia if I 'appen to stop a lump of lead, sir—that's what's worryin' me." Life in Australia meant riding on horseback when he was not following at the plough's tail. It was the only life he knew, and he loved it. But I was fully convinced that he no more feared actual death than he feared a mosquito, and when he left the ship at Suez, and joined lustily in the singing of "Australia will be there"—who so jovial as he? He got through the fighting on Gallipoli, only to be destroyed on the Somme; his horse, if it had not already been sent to Palestine, had to submit to another rider; his acres to produce for another ploughman.

The last illness is, of course, sometimes very unpleasant, especially if cancer or angina pectoris enter into the picture, but I have often marvelled at the endurance of men who should, according to all one's preconceived ideas, be broken up with distress. Not uncommonly a man refuses to believe that he is really so seriously ill as other people think, and there is always the hope eternal in every breast that he will get better. Quite commonly he looks hopefully in the glass every morning as he shaves for signs of coming improvement; there are few men who really believe that sentence of early death has been passed upon them.

The illness which causes the most misery is an illness complicated with neurasthenia, and probably the neurasthenic tastes the bitterest misery of which mankind is capable, unless we admit melancholia into the grisly competition. But I often think that the long sleepless early morning hours of neurasthenia, when the patient lies listening for the chimes, worrying over his physical condition and harassed with dread of the future, are the most terrible possible to man. Nor are they in any way improved by the knowledge that sometimes neurasthenia does not indicate any real physical disease.

But it is difficult to find any really rational cause for the desire to live longer, unless Sir Thomas Browne is right in thinking that the long habit of living indisposeth us for dying. After all, what does it really matter whether we die to-morrow or live twenty more years? In another century it will be all the same; at most we but postpone dissolution. Death has to come sooner or later; and whatever we believe of our life beyond the grave is not likely to make any difference. We were not consulted as to whether we were to be born, nor as to the parts and capabilities which were to be allotted to us, and it is exceedingly unlikely that our wishes will be taken into consideration as regards our eternal disposition. We can do no more when we come to die than take our involuntary leap into the dark like innumerable living creatures before us, and, conscious of having done our duty to the best that lay in us, hope for the best.

Twentieth-century biological science appears to result in a kind of vague pantheism, coupled with a generous hedonism. Scientific men appear to find their pleasure, not like the old Greeks, sought by each man for himself, but rather in "the greatest happiness of the greatest number." It is difficult for a modern man to feel entirely happy while he knows of the vast amount of incurable misery that exists in the world. The idea of Heaven is simply an idea that the atrocious injustice and unhappiness of life in this world must be balanced by equally great happiness in the life to come; but is there any evidence to favour such a belief? Is there any evidence throughout Nature that the spirit of justice is anything but a dream of man himself which is never to be fulfilled? We do not like to speak of "death," but prefer rather to avoid the hated term by some journalistic periphrasis, such as "solved the great enigma." But is there any enigma? Or are we going to solve it? Is it not more likely that our protoplasm is destined to become dissolved into its primordial electrons, and ultimately to be lost in the general ocean of ether, and that when we die we shall solve no enigma, because there is no enigma to solve?

To sum up, death probably does not hurt nearly so much as the ordinary sufferings which are the lot of everybody in living; the act of death is probably no more terrible than our nightly falling asleep; and probably the condition of everlasting rest is what Fate has in store for us, and we can face it bravely without flinching when our time comes. But whether we flinch or not will not matter; we have to die all the same, and we shall be less likely to flinch if we can feel that we have tried to do our duty. And what are we to say of a man who has seen his duty, and urgently longed to perform it, but has failed because God has not given him sufficient strength? "Video meliora proboque, deteriora sequor," as old Cicero said of himself. If there is any enigma at all, it lies in the frustrated longings and bitter disappointment of that man.

Probably the best shield throughout life against the atrocious evils and injustices which every man has to suffer is a kind of humorous fatalism which holds that other people have suffered as much as ourselves; that such suffering is a necessary concomitant of life upon this world; and that nothing much matters so long as we do our duty in the sphere to which Fate has called us. A kindly irony which enables us to laugh at the world and sympathize with its troubles is a very powerful aid in the battle; and if a doctor does his part in alleviating pain and postponing death—if he does his best for rich and poor, and always listens to the cry of the afflicted,—and if he endeavours to leave his wife and children in a position better than he himself began, I do not see what more can be expected of him either in this world or the next. And probably Huxley was not far wrong when he said: "I have no faith, very little hope, and as much charity as I can afford." It is amazing that there are some people in the world to-day who look upon a man who professes these merciful sentiments as a miscreant doomed to eternal flames because he will not profess to believe in their own particular form of religion. They think they have answered him when they proclaim that his creed is sterile.

as regards our eternal disposition. We can do no more when we come to die than take our involuntary leap into the dark like innumerable living creatures before us, and, conscious of having done our duty to the best that lay in us, hope for the best.

Twentieth-century biological science appears to result in a kind of vague pantheism, coupled with a generous hedonism. Scientific men appear to find their pleasure, not like the old Greeks, sought by each man for himself, but rather in "the greatest happiness of the greatest number." It is difficult for a modern man to feel entirely happy while he knows of the vast amount of incurable misery that exists in the world. The idea of Heaven is simply an idea that the atrocious injustice and unhappiness of life in this world must be balanced by equally great happiness in the life to come; but is there any evidence to favour such a belief? Is there any evidence throughout Nature that the spirit of justice is anything but a dream of man himself which is never to be fulfilled? We do not like to speak of "death," but prefer rather to avoid the hated term by some journalistic periphrasis, such as "solved the great enigma." But is there any enigma? Or are we going to solve it? Is it not more likely that our protoplasm is destined to become dissolved into its primordial electrons, and ultimately to be lost in the general ocean of ether, and that when we die we shall solve no enigma, because there is no enigma to solve?

To sum up, death probably does not hurt nearly so much as the ordinary sufferings which are the lot of everybody in living; the act of death is probably no more terrible than our nightly falling asleep; and probably the condition of everlasting rest is what Fate has in store for us, and we can face it bravely without flinching when our time comes. But whether we flinch or not will not matter; we have to die all the same, and we shall be less likely to flinch if we can feel that we have tried to do our duty. And what are we to say of a man who has seen his duty, and urgently longed to perform it, but has failed because God has not given him sufficient strength? "Video meliora proboque, deteriora sequor," as old Cicero said of himself. If there is any enigma at all, it lies in the frustrated longings and bitter disappointment of that man.

Probably the best shield throughout life against the atrocious evils and injustices which every man has to suffer is a kind of humorous fatalism which holds that other people have suffered as much as ourselves; that such suffering is a necessary concomitant of life upon this world; and that nothing much matters so long as we do our duty in the sphere to which Fate has called us. A kindly irony which enables us to laugh at the world and sympathize with its troubles is a very powerful aid in the battle; and if a doctor does his part in alleviating pain and postponing death—if he does

FOOTNOTES:

[1] I have read or heard that one of the charges against Cardinal Wolsey was that he had given the King syphilis by whispering in his ear. The nature of the story so whispered is not disclosed, but may be imagined. But the proud prelate had several perfectly healthy illegitimate children, and on the whole it is probable that Henry caught the disease in the usual way.

[2] They really seem to have taken some little pains to make the death of the King's old flame as little terrible as possible. They might have burnt her or subjected her to the usual grim preliminaries of the scaffold. Probably they did this not because the King had ever loved her, but because she was a queen, and therefore not to be subjected to needless infamy; one of the Lord's anointed, in short.

[3] To pause for a moment, probably the element of human sacrifice may have entered into the hair-cutting episode, as it did in the action of the women of Carthage during the last siege; and possibly there may have been some shamefaced reserve in the attributing of the fashion to the example of an egregious "Buster Brown" of New York. To my own memory the fashion was first called either the "Joan of Arc" cut or the "Munitioner" cut. The "Buster Brown" cut came later, and seems to have been seized upon by the English as an excuse against showing deep feelings. It is pleasanter to think that Joan of Arc was really at that time in the hearts of English women; the cult of semi-worship that so strengthened the Allies was really worship of the qualities which mankind has read into the memory of the little maid of Domremy. As she raised the siege of Orleans, so her memory encouraged the Allies to persevere through years of agony nearly as great as her own.

[4] We can see from the statues of Jeanne d'Arc how near akin are the sex-complex and the art-complex. I do not refer to the innumerable pretty statues scattered throughout the French churches, which are merely ideal portraits of sainted women. The magnificent equestrian statue by Fremiet in the Place des Pyramides, Paris, is a portrait of a plump little French peasant-girl trying to look fierce, and succeeding about as well as Audrey might if she tried to play Lady Macbeth. But it is essentially female, and, in my idea of Jeanne d'Arc, is therefore wrong, for we really know nothing about her beyond what we read in the trials. Even more female is the statue of her by

Romaneill in the Melbourne Art Gallery, in which the artist has actually depicted the corslet as curved to accommodate moderate-sized breasts, a thing which would probably have shocked Jeanne herself, for she wished to make herself sexually unattractive. The face, though common, is probably accurate in that it depicts her expression as saintly. No doubt when she was listening to her Voices she did look dreamy and ethereal. But we have no authority for believing that she was in the slightest degree beautiful—if anything, she was probably rather the reverse.

[5] I hate to suggest that these specks before the eyes may have been the result of toxæmia from the intestine induced by confinement and terror.

[6] Grotius was the Dutchman who could write Latin verse at the age of nine, and had to leave Holland because of fierce theological strife. He began the study for his great work on the laws of war in prison, from which he escaped by the remarkable loyalty of his wife. Like so many romantic episodes, fiction is here anticipated by fact.

[7] Sir W. Stirling-Maxwell, *The Cloister Life of Charles V.*

[8] It has been thought that she suffered from "phantom-tumour"— "pseudo-cyesis" in medical language.

[9] Dr. Gordon Davidson, a well-known ophthalmic surgeon of Sydney, thinks that Pepys probably suffered from iridocyclitis, the result of some toxæmia, possibly caused by his extreme imprudence in eating and drinking.